Selected Poems

A.D. HOPE

Selected Poems

Chosen and Introduced by
RUTH MORSE

First published in 1986 by
Carcanet Press Limited

British Library Cataloguing in Publication Data
Hope. A.D. (Alec Derwent)
Selected Poems.
I. Title   II. Morse, Ruth
821   PR6015.0597

ISBN 0-85635-640-9

This book should not under any circumstances be
rebound in hardback form.

The Publisher acknowledges the financial assistance
of the Arts Council of Great Britain.

Printed digitally since 2001.
Carcanet Press Limited, *now at* Conavon Court, Blackfriar Street
Manchester M3 5BQ UK   www.carcanet.co.uk

Contents

Introduction

ALEC DERWENT HOPE was born in Cooma, New South Wales, in 1907, the eldest of five children. In 1911 his father, a Presbyterian minister, moved with his family to a congregation in Tasmania; his modest salary was supplemented by a small farm, to which his parishioners contributed their labour. "Hay Fever" recalls the young Hope's first experience of mowing, an experience which country boys still had up until the end of the Second World War. Rural Tasmania in the Edwardian period was a quiet outpost of the British Empire, and that country childhood was more like its English Non-Conformist equivalent than it would ever be again. Hope was taught to read and write by his mother, and learned rudimentary Latin from his father. School, when there were enough children in the area to warrant organizing one, was held in the local shearing shed, except, of course, when it was needed for the sheep. The Hopes' library consisted of the classics of English literature, especially poetry, and the parents took it in turn to read aloud to the children. Spenser, Milton, the great Romantic and Victorian poets were Hope's earliest reading. At eight he wrote his first long poem, a 52-stanza birthday present for his mother, exhorting her in her Christian duty, week by week. He remembers that she had the tact not to laugh, and that she thanked him for his gift, reminding him that he, too, might need to think about his own duty.

Like so many other clever children of the era, Hope was sent back to the Australian mainland for more formal schooling when he was fourteen; he boarded with family friends while he studied at Bathurst High School. The verse he wrote then was ceremoniously burned on the advice of an older friend. From Bathurst he gained a place at Fort Street High School, one of Sydney's best selective schools. He wanted to study medicine at University, but his science results were not good enough, though he won a scholarship reserved for the sons of Presbyterian clergy, to St Andrew's College of the University of Sydney, to read for an Arts degree. This early interest in science has provided him with subjects throughout his writing life. His poetry appeared in several Sydney University magazines, and he published one poem in *The Bulletin* when he was twenty. Though the early poetry gives no hint of the quality of what was to come, it does introduce a strong impression of continuity in Hope's interests. It shows knowledge of French poets as well as English models. Like most of his contemporaries, he wrote in formal metres, as he has continued to do. The metrical experiments of this period anticipate his ambition to write a long, conversational line which would extend the normal English pentameter; he was heavily influenced by Swinburne. This absorption in the traditions of poetry and drama can also be seen in one long collaborative effort which survives in the archives of Sydney University: a masque written as a celebration of a university occasion. Ten years after the Great War Sydney was still a provincial place; the population of all of Australia was under six million, almost without exception of British (including then Irish) descent. Censorship determined what books they would be allowed to read; they looked back to Britain as a model. Hope distinguished himself as an undergraduate, coming top of his year in both philosophy and English, and won another scholarship, this time to England. Again, like many other clever young men, he set off to complete his education, if not a wild, certainly a colonial, boy.

In 1928 he went to University College, Oxford, to read English. Auden and his generation had just gone down. Hope was poor, ill at ease, and under-prepared. His letters home describe the grind of preparing the highly philological course which was Oxford English of the period: Anglo-Saxon, Old Norse, Gothic, and a little medieval literature. He spent his vacations with friends, postponed the hard work he kept promising himself, and finally left Oxford with a third-class degree. The experience confirmed his respect for specialist scholarship – he was taught both by C.S. Lewis and by the editor of *Beowulf*, C.L. Wrenn – while convincing him that he was himself no scholar. Something of his sympathy for the scholar's life is recorded in "Meditation on a Bone", which at the same time encapsulates a perception of its limitations. He had to borrow the money to pay his passage home, and could not even afford to leave the conventional deposit to pay for his M.A.

Hope returned to Sydney at the beginning of the Depression, with no prospects, and little ambition beyond finding a job that would allow him to get on with writing poetry. He taught school briefly and badly, and spent as much of his time as he could camping at the coast and learning Russian. For five years he worked as a vocational psychologist and then as a school counsellor. He published a few poems in Australian little magazines, and began to make a name for himself as a witty and uncompromising reviewer. From 1937-44 he lectured at the Sydney Teachers' College, then in 1945 moved to a senior lectureship at the University of Melbourne. There he taught English and European literature; students of the time recall that he seemed almost to be talking to himself when he lectured on Dante or the Russian novel, or Dryden, or numerous Australian writers, with a quiet authority that filled them with enthusiasm. He was an early supporter of the teaching of Australian literature in Australian universities.

In 1951 he became the first Professor of English at the new Canberra University College, now the Australian National University, a chair which he held for seventeen years. While the new English department was still in temporary quarters a fire there destroyed his library, lecture notes, correspondence, and manuscripts. Ironically, he had just moved all his papers into his office so that they would be safe while he moved house. This inadvertent conflagration means that very little of his early work survives.

The manuscript of Hope's first collection escaped the fire, and *The Wandering Islands* appeared in 1955, when he was forty-eight. Some of the poems had been published in university reviews and little magazines, and more of them had circulated in manuscript. In the parochial atmosphere of Australia in the fifties – still bound by the censorship of thirty years before – the book caused a sensation. The shock of Hope's sexual explicitness and the ferocity of his wit scandalized many readers; some reacted to his elegant formalism with accusations of a sterile academicism; his learning and allusiveness led others to condemn him for deliberate obscurity, despite the clarity which characterizes his poetry. His verse looked European, and therefore, to many of his countrymen, anti-Australian, a view which was given currency by some of the satires, especially "Australia", which was for many years the only poem he published which was explicitly connected to his country. These have remained the general areas of criticism of his work, and he has been stigmatized as an Augustan, a Romantic, a Nietzschean, a Manichee, and latterly an elitist and a misogynist. The list of accusations is perhaps a compliment to a poet who has always aroused strong feelings, and to a poet who has something to say.

Hope's characteristic eroticism depends upon complex perceptions of man's place in creation. Not only is his own life ephemeral, but his relation to generation is a contingent one; it is women who are the ultimate creators, who bear the burden as well as the ultimate mystery of life. Like other love poets, Hope writes of the search for the self in the unknown beloved, of complementarity and the urge for completion that can never be satisfied. His *personae* approach his central concerns from a variety of points of view; it is not surprising that those who have tried to construct a coherent philosophy from the poetry have found it a tangle of contradictions. The central core, the base on which other experience depends, is sexuality in the widest sense. From the intensity of sexuality Hope moves in several directions. One is towards an understanding of the natural role of the power of sexuality, which, in humanity as in other species, is to ensure continuation of the race. Nature's indifference to the individual can be a source of loneliness, even despair, as in "The Death of the Bird", but it can also provoke an amused tolerance, as in the late "The Invaders". Nature's fecundity can provide a source of celebration, as in "Standardization", which is often dismissed simply as satire, or in many poems in which the artist's participation in the mystery of creation comes to be seen as a parallel to the central sexual mystery and its necessary consequence, the creation of new life. "On an Engraving of Casserius" brings these themes together. Even Hope's most discursive, meditative poems are firmly anchored in the experience of individual speakers. This is marked in the dramatic monologue placed in the mouth of the seventeenth-century figure, Sir Edward Sackville, whose thoughts take him from the intensity of his own experience of love and loss to more general reflections of the place of love in nature. Similarly, the twentieth-century lover who speaks the "Mu'allaqat of Murray's Corner" transfers pre-Islamic poetic conventions (the "mu'allaqats" were a series of famous Odes which were copied out and displayed in the Caliph's palace) to an Australian landscape to consider the implications of his personal experience of loss, relating it first to the poetic subject of the earlier, Arab poet, Imr Al-Qais, then to more universal themes. Peter Abelard, the medieval French philosopher, is another historical figure whom Hope has pressed into service for his explorations. By the time of the late poem, "The Drifting Continent", the eroticism is almost entirely subordinated to the general questions about the future of mankind. The poet's celebration is never unalloyed rejoicing, but however central "loss" has been to Hope as a subject, he has more tones than the elegiac, as the mathematical jokes of "Möbius Strip-Tease" or the wit of the satires show.

Particularly for Australian readers, Hope's learning has been an obstacle. In no country of the English speaking world is the education which gave the child of the rural Tasmanian manse access to the traditions of western culture any longer taken for granted; on the contrary, hostility to that education is a feature of many of the mass democracies, where it is identified with the colonial experience and the rule of the Empire. As a child, before and during the Great War, Hope absorbed Latin poetry, with its rich mythology, along with the Bible's stories, cadences, and imagery, and those traditions have provided him with resources throughout his life. Each of the poems which uses that heritage adds something to it; he sees the old stories from a new point of view. He shows Ulysses ("The End of a Journey") or Persephone ("The Return of Persephone") at the moment of realizing something about their experience. In "The Muse", one of his few poems which directly addresses poetic creativity, he offers a view which suggests that his own experience differs from that of his friend and fellow-poet, James McAuley, to whom "The Muse" is a reply. In this poem, too, we see an instance of his commitment to the idea that poets, like musicians, can write themes and variations. Not only does he use and revivify the myths referred to in McAuley's similarly titled poem, but he imitates McAuley's form, like

Raleigh or Donne or Day Lewis replying to Marlowe's "Passionate Shepherd to his Love." Hope's variations on Biblical stories also show his independent interpretation of what tradition provides; the best-known instance of this is the often-anthologized "Imperial Adam." Because the Bible remains fairly well-known, in whatever version, such poems remain easy of access, whether they deal with Lot and his family or with the Apocryphal tale of Susanna and the Elders, also the subject of a poem by Wallace Stevens. A third broad area of inspiration, not always thought of as coherent in the same way as the Classical or the Judaeo-Christian legacies, is the tradition of western literature. Hope has often added to the legends created by earlier writers. "Man Friday" looks at Defoe's *Robinson Crusoe*; Marlowe's play is behind "Faustus"; John Skelton provides the title and epigraph for "Speak, Parrot!"; Byron inspired one of the most conversational of Hope's poems, "A Letter from Rome." This long, familiar letter deals directly with the weight of our artistic heritage, and with Hope's own relationship to it as a twentieth-century Australian. The idea of our literature as a conversation is one that he finds essential; he himself has taken high culture, if not for granted, at least as the birthright of any educated person who is interested in it. To many of his countrymen, his bookishness has seemed at best an act of defiance, at worst a betrayal. If Hope, who has spent his life in the country of his birth, sometimes seems to them a transplanted European, that is perhaps best seen as Europe's good luck, however much such a notion may jar against post-colonial ideas of a national literature expressed in a distinctively Australian idiom.

The language of Hope's poetry is – despite the difficulty of definition – best described as standard English; he uses few words that would immediately identify him as an Australian, though this selection includes an Australian vernacular translation of a drinking poem from the Greek Anthology (also translated by Cowley), and "Möbius Strip-Tease", which belongs to the ballad tradition, always strong in Australia, as well as "The Drifting Continent." While Hope modulates down for comic effect, he is prone to modulate up, to use unusual or archaic words if they suit the style of a particular poem; one consistent idiosyncrasy is the retention of "still" to mean "always." The general effect is a kind of elevated conversational tone: the lines give the impression of a speaking voice, but are often more formal or complex than an actual speaker would be. While his syntax exploits normal English order, his adherence to formal metres gives him the added resources of traditional rhythm and rhyme. Hope's achievement belongs to the line of poetry in English which includes Yeats and Frost. Like theirs, his eloquence stems from an elegant simplicity which conveys remarkable emotional power. Yet it must be added that there is a great deal of informal poetry, some of which was collected in *Antechinus*, but much of which remains unpublished. In old age Hope has continued to experiment, as with "The Western Elegies", which cross the Latin hexameter with the English alliterative long line, and "Ladies from the Sea", his first full-length play. In making a selection from the length of A.D. Hope's career, I have sought to create a balance between the often-anthologized and the less well-known, the early and the late, his satires, love poetry, and discursive, contemplative poems. There has been space for only one extended piece, which has meant the omission not only of any part of *The New Dunciad*, but also the most recent narrative verse. "A Mu'allaqat of Murray's Corner", "Eyes and Tongues", and the translation from Florbela Espanca, appear for the first time; "The Mayan Books", the translation from the Greek Anthology, and "Möbius Strip-Tease" appear in book form for the first time. No one will be satisfied by the choices, and that is as it should be; there is more good poetry than a volume of this size will accommodate. The poems are arranged in chronological order, following Hope's usual habit.

A.D. Hope has published a dozen volumes of verse, including two previous *Selected Poems* and two editions of his *Collected Poems*, the most recent of which is now fifteen years old. Since that volume appeared, he has published *A Late Picking* (1975); *A Book of Answers* (1978); *The Drifting Continent* (1979); which was absorbed in *Antechinus* (1981); *The Tragical History of Dr Faustus* (1982), an adaptation of Marlowe's play; and *The Age of Reason* (1985), a collection of verse narratives. His essays have been collected in three volumes: *The Cave and the Spring* (1965), *Native Companions* (1974), and *The Pack of Autolycus* (1979). He is the author of books on the Scots poet William Dunbar, *A Midsummer Eve's Dream* (1970); on *Judith Wright* (1975); and on the writing of poetry, *The New Cratylus* (1979). Among his awards for poetry are the Grace Levin Prize (1956), the Arts Council of Great Britain Award (1965), the Volkswagen Award (1966), the Myer Award (1967), the Levinson Prize (1969), the Ingram Merrill Award (1969), and the Robert Frost Award (1976). He was the first Library Fellow of the Australian National University, and still keeps an office in the English department there. He received the O.B.E. in 1972 and the A.C. in 1981. In 1985 he was elected Ashby Visiting Fellow of Clare Hall, Cambridge, and Honorary Fellow of University College, Oxford. In 1937 he married Penelope Robinson; they live in Canberra near their two sons.

For this selection printed texts of the poems have been collated with the manuscripts in the Australian National Library and in the poet's possession. A very few textual changes have been made, mainly to restore original punctuation and to correct inevitable errors of transcription; all have been made with the poet's approval. The editor wishes to

12

thank the Manuscripts Librarian and Mr James Rigney of the Fisher Library, University of Sydney; Mrs Pamela Ray and her staff of the Australian National Library; the Humanities Research Centre of the Australian National University; the Fryer Memorial Library of the University of Queensland; and the British Academy, which made her trip to Australia possible. Special thanks are due to Mike and Lyb Hillman, and to Bill Ramson and Joan Hughes, whose educative and recuperative efforts provided a constant and inspiriting example.

Ruth Morse
Clare Hall, Cambridge
July 1985

To Andrew and Geoffrey

The End of a Journey

There at the last, his arms embracing her,
She found herself, faith wasted, valour lost,
Raped by a stranger in her sullen bed;
And he, for all the bloody passion it cost
To have heard the sirens sing and yet have fled,
Thought the night tedious, coughed and shook his head,
An old man sleeping with his housekeeper.

But with the dawn he rose and stepped outside.
A farm-cart by the doorway dripped and stank,
Piled with the victims of his mighty bow.
Each with her broken neck, each with a blank,
Small, strangled face, the dead girls in a row
Swung as the cold airs moved them to and fro,
Full-breasted, delicate-waisted, heavy-thighed.

Setting his jaw, he turned and clambered down
A goat-track to the beach: the tide was full.
He stood and brooded on the breaking wave
Revolving many memories in his skull:
Calypso singing in her haunted cave,
The bed of Circe, Hector in his grave
And Priam butchered in his burning town.

Grimly he watched his enemy the sea
Rage round the petty kingdom he called home;
But now no trident threatened from the spray.
He prayed, but knew Athene would not come.
The gods at last had left him, and the day
Darkened about him. Then from far away
And long ago, he seemed once more to be

Roped to a mast and through the breakers' roar
Sweet voices mocked him on his reeling deck:
"Son of Laertes, what delusive song
Turned your swift keel and brought you to this wreck,
In age and disenchantment to prolong
Stale years and chew the cud of ancient wrong,
A castaway upon so cruel a shore?"

Standardization

When, darkly brooding on this Modern Age,
The journalist with his marketable woes
Fills up once more the inevitable page
Of fatuous, flatulent, Sunday-paper prose;

Whenever the green aesthete starts to whoop
With horror at the house not made with hands
And when from vacuum cleaners and tinned soup
Another pure theosophist demands

Rebirth in other, less industrial stars
Where huge towns thrust up in synthetic stone
And films and sleek miraculous motor cars
And celluloid and rubber are unknown;

When from his vegetable Sunday School
Emerges with the neatly maudlin phrase
Still one more Nature poet, to rant or drool
About the "Standardization of the Race";

I see, stooping among her orchard trees,
The old, sound Earth, gathering her windfalls in,
Broad in the hams and stiffening at the knees,
Pause and I see her grave malicious grin.

For there is no manufacturer competes
With her in the mass production of shapes and things.
Over and over she gathers and repeats
The cast of a face, a million butterfly wings.

She does not tire of the pattern of a rose.
Her oldest tricks still catch us with surprise.
She cannot recall how long ago she chose
The streamlined hulls of fish, the snail's long eyes,

Love, which still pours into its ancient mould
The lashing seed that grows to a man again,
From whom by the same processes unfold
Unending generations of living men.

She has standardized his ultimate needs and pains.
Lost tribes in a lost language mutter in
His dreams: his science is tethered to their brains,
His guilt merely repeats Original Sin.

And beauty standing motionless before
Her mirror sees behind her, mile on mile,
A long queue in an unknown corridor,
Anonymous faces plastered with her smile.

Australia

A Nation of trees, drab green and desolate grey
In the field uniform of modern wars,
Darkens her hills, those endless, outstretched paws
Of Sphinx demolished or stone lion worn away.

They call her a young country, but they lie:
She is the last of lands, the emptiest,
A woman beyond her change of life, a breast
Still tender but within the womb is dry.

Without songs, architecture, history:
The emotions and superstitions of younger lands,
Her rivers of water drown among inland sands,
The river of her immense stupidity

Floods her monotonous tribes from Cairns to Perth.
In them at last the ultimate men arrive
Whose boast is not: "we live" but "we survive",
A type who will inhabit the dying earth.

And her five cities, like five teeming sores,
Each drains her: a vast parasite robber-state
Where second-hand Europeans pullulate
Timidly on the edge of alien shores.

Yet there are some like me turn gladly home
From the lush jungle of modern thought, to find
The Arabian desert of the human mind,
Hoping, if still from the deserts the prophets come,

Such savage and scarlet as no green hills dare
Springs in that waste, some spirit which escapes
The learned doubt, the chatter of cultured apes
Which is called civilization over there.

Observation Car

To be put on the train and kissed and given my ticket,
Then the station slid backward, the shops and the neon lighting,
Reeling off in a drunken blur, with a whole pound note in my
    pocket
And the holiday packed with Perhaps. It used to be very exciting.

The present and past were enough. I did not mind having my back
To the engine. I sat like a spider and spun
Time backward out of my guts – or rather my eyes – and the track
Was a Now dwindling off to oblivion. I thought it was fun:

The telegraph poles slithered up in a sudden crescendo
As we sliced the hill and scattered its grazing sheep;
The days were a wheeling delirium that led without end to
Nights when we plunged into roaring tunnels of sleep.

But now I am tired of the train. I have learned that one tree
Is much like another, one hill the dead spit of the next
I have seen tailing off behind all the various types of country
Like a clock running down. I am bored and a little perplexed;

And weak with the effort of endless evacuation
Of the long monotonous Now, the repetitive, tidy
Officialdom of each siding, of each little station
Labelled Monday, Tuesday – and goodness! what happened to
Friday?

And the maddening way the other passengers alter:
The schoolgirl who goes to the Ladies' comes back to her seat
A lollipop blonde who leads you on to assault her,
And you've just got her skirts round her waist and her pants
round her feet

When you find yourself fumbling about the nightmare knees
Of a pink hippopotamus with a permanent wave
Who sends you for sandwiches and a couple of teas,
But by then she has whiskers, no teeth and one foot in the grave.

I have lost my faith that the ticket tells where we are going.
There are rumours the driver is mad – we are all being trucked
To the abattoirs somewhere – the signals are jammed and
unknowing
We aim through the night full speed at a wrecked viaduct.

But I do not believe them. The future is rumour and drivel;
Only the past is assured. From the observation car
I stand looking back and watching the landscape shrivel,
Wondering where we are going and just where the hell we are,

Remembering how I planned to break the journey, to drive
My own car one day, to have choice in my hands and my foot
upon power,
To see through the trumpet throat of vertiginous perspective
My urgent Now explode continually into flower,

To be the Eater of Time, a poet and not that sly
Anus of mind the historian. It was so simple and plain
To live by the sole, insatiable influx of the eye.
But something went wrong with the plan: I am still on the train.

The Gateway

Now the heart sings with all its thousand voices
To hear this city of cells, my body, sing.
The tree through the stiff clay at long last forces
Its thin strong roots and taps the secret spring.

And the sweet waters without intermission
Climb to the tips of its green tenement;
The breasts have borne the grace of their possession,
The lips have felt the pressure of content.

Here I come home: in this expected country
They know my name and speak it with delight.
I am the dream and you my gates of entry,
The means by which I waken into light.

The Wandering Islands

You cannot build bridges between the wandering islands;
The Mind has no neighbours, and the unteachable heart
Announces its armistice time after time, but spends
Its love to draw them closer and closer apart.

They are not on the chart; they turn indifferent shoulders
On the island-hunters; they are not afraid
Of Cook or De Quiros, nor of the empire-builders;
By missionary bishops and the tourist trade

They are not annexed; they claim no fixed position;
They take no pride in a favoured latitude;
The committee of atolls inspires in them no devotion
And the earthquake belt no special attitude.

A refuge only for the shipwrecked sailor;
He sits on the shore and sullenly masturbates,
Dreaming of rescue, the pubs in the ports of call or
The big-hipped harlots at the dockyard gates.

But the wandering islands drift on their own business,
Incurious whether the whales swim round or under,
Investing no fear in ultimate forgiveness.
If they clap together, it is only casual thunder

And yet they are hurt – for the social polyps never
Girdle their bare shores with a moral reef;
When the icebergs grind them they know both beauty and terror;
They are not exempt from ordinary grief;

And the sudden ravages of love surprise
Them like acts of God – its irresistible function
They have never treated with convenient lies
As a part of geography or an institution.

An instant of fury, a bursting mountain of spray,
They rush together, their promontories lock,
An instant the castaway hails the castaway,
But the sounds perish in that earthquake shock.

And then, in the crash of ruined cliffs, the smother
And swirl of foam, the wandering islands part.
But all that one mind ever knows of another,
Or breaks the long isolation of the heart,

Was in that instant. The shipwrecked sailor senses
His own despair in a retreating face.
Around him he hears in the huge monotonous voices
Of wave and wind: "The Rescue will not take place."

Ascent Into Hell

Little Henry, too, had a great notion of singing.
– HISTORY OF THE FAIRCHILD FAMILY

I, too, at the mid-point, in a well-lit wood
Of second-rate purpose and mediocre success,
Explore in dreams the never-never of childhood,
Groping in daylight for the key of darkness;

He cannot turn back, a lurking horror beckons
Round the next corner, beyond each further door.
Sweating with nameless anguish then he wakens;
Finds the familiar walls blank as before.

Chased by wild bulls, his legs stick fast with terror.
He reaches the fence at last – the fence falls flat.
Choking, he runs, the trees he climbs will totter.
Or the cruel horns, like telescopes, shoot out.

At his fourth year the waking life turns inward.
Here on his Easter Island the stone faces
Rear meaningless monuments of hate and dread.
Dreamlike within the dream real names and places

Survive. His mother comforts him with her body
Against the nightmare of the lions and tigers.
Again he is standing in his father's study
Lying about his lie, is whipped, and hears

His scream of outrage, valid to this day.
In bed, he fingers his stump of sex, invents
How he took off his clothes and ran away,
Slit up his belly with various instruments;

To brood on this was a deep abdominal joy
Still recognized as a feeling at the core
Of love – and the last genuine memory
Is singing "Jesus Loves Me" – then, no more!

Beyond is a lost country and in vain
I enter that mysterious territory.
Lit by faint hints of memory lies the plain
Where from its Null took shape this conscious I

Revisit, among the morning archipelagoes,
Tasmania, my receding childish island;
Unchanged my prehistoric flora grows
Within me, marsupial territories extend:

22

There is the land-locked valley and the river,
The Western Tiers make distance an emotion,
The gum trees roar in the gale, the poplars shiver
At twilight, the church pines imitate an ocean.

There, in the clear night, still I listen, waking
To a crunch of sulky wheels on the distant road;
The marsh of stars reflects a starry croaking;
I hear in the pillow the sobbing of my blood

As the panic of unknown footsteps marching nearer,
Till the door opens, the inner world of panic
Nightmares that woke me to unawakening terror
Birthward resume their still inscrutable traffic.

Memory no more the backward, solid continent,
From island to island of despairing dream
I follow the dwindling soul in its ascent;
The bayonets and the pickelhauben gleam

Among the leaves, as, in the poplar tree,
They find him hiding. With an axe he stands
Above the German soldiers, hopelessly
Chopping the fingers from the climbing hands.

Or, in the well-known house, a secret door
Opens on empty rooms from which a stair
Leads down to a grey, dusty corridor,
Room after room, ominous, still and bare.

Which backward scans the dark – But at my side
The unrecognized Other Voice speaks in my ear,
The voice of my fear, the voice of my unseen guide;
"Who are we, stranger? What are we doing here?"

And through the uncertain gloom, sudden I see
Beyond remembered time the imagined entry,
The enormous Birth-gate whispering, *"per me,
per me si va tra la perduta gente."*

Conquistador

I sing of the decline of Henry Clay
Who loved a white girl of uncommon size.
Although a small man in a little way,
He had in him some seed of enterprise.

Each day he caught the seven-thirty train
To work, watered his garden after tea,
Took an umbrella if it looked like rain
And was remarkably like you or me.

He had his hair cut once a fortnight, tried
Not to forget the birthday of his wife,
And might have lived unnoticed till he died
Had not ambition entered Henry's life.

He met her in the lounge of an hotel
– A most unusual place for him to go –
But there he was and there she was as well,
Sitting alone. He ordered beers for two.

She was so large a girl that when they came
He gave the waiter twice the usual tip.
She smiled without surprise, told him her name,
And as the name trembled on Henry's lip,

His parched soul, swelling like a desert root,
Broke out its delicate dream upon the air;
The mountains shook with earthquake under foot;
An angel seized him suddenly by the hair;

The sky was shrill with peril as he passed;
A hurricane crushed his senses with its din;
The wildfire crackled up his reeling mast;
The trumpet of a maelstrom sucked him in;

The desert shrivelled and burnt off his feet;
His bones and buttons an enormous snake
Vomited up; still in the shimmering heat
The pygmies showed him their forbidden lake

And then transfixed him with their poison darts;
He married six black virgins in a bunch,
Who, when they had drawn out his manly parts,
Stewed him and ate him lovingly for lunch.

Adventure opened wide its grisly jaws;
Henry looked in and knew the Hero's doom.
The huge white girl drank on without a pause
And, just at closing time, she asked him home.

The tram they took was full of Roaring Boys
Announcing the world's ruin and Judgement Day;
The sky blared with its grand orchestral voice
The Götterdämmerung of Henry Clay.

But in her quiet room they were alone.
There, towering over Henry by a head,
She stood and took her clothes off one by one,
And then she stretched herself upon the bed.

Her bulk of beauty, her stupendous grace
Challenged the lion heart in his puny dust.
Proudly his Moment looked him in the face:
He rose to meet it as a hero must;

Climbed the white mountain of unravished snow,
Planted his tiny flag upon the peak.
The smooth drifts, scarcely breathing, lay below.
She did not take the trouble to smile or speak.

And afterwards, it may have been in play,
The enormous girl rolled over and squashed him flat;
And, as she could not send him home that way,
Used him thereafter as a bedside mat.

Speaking at large, I will say this of her:
She did not spare expense to make him nice.
Tanned on both sides and neatly edged with fur,
The job would have been cheap at any price.

And when, in winter, getting out of bed,
Her large soft feet pressed warmly on the skin,
The two glass eyes would sparkle in his head,
The jaws extend their papier-mâché grin.

Good people, for the soul of Henry Clay
Offer your prayers, and view his destiny!
He was the Hero of our Time. He may
With any luck, one day, be you or me.

The Lingam and the Yoni

The Lingam and the Yoni
Are walking hand in glove,
O are you listening, honey?
I hear my honey-love.

The He and She our movers
What is it they discuss?
Is it the talk of Lovers?
And do they speak of us?

I hear their high palaver –
O tell me what they say!
The talk goes on for ever
So deep in love are they;

So deep in thought, debating
The suburb and the street;
Time-payment calculating
Upon the bedroom suite.

But ours is long division
By love's arithmetic,
Until they make provision
To buy a box of brick,

A box that makes her prisoner,
That he must slave to win
To do the Lingam honour,
To keep the Yoni in.

The mortgage on tomorrow?
The haemorrhage of rent?
Against the heart they borrow
At five or six per cent.

The heart has bought fulfilment
Which yet their mouths defer
Until the last instalment
Upon the furniture.

No Lingam for her money
Can make up youth's arrears:
His layby on the Yoni
Will not be paid in years.

And they, who keep this tally,
They count what they destroy;
While, in its secret valley
Withers the herb of joy.

X-Ray Photograph

Mapped by its panoply of shade
There is the skull I shall not see
– Dark hollow in its galaxy
From which the blazing eye must fade –

And, though I cannot see it plain,
Within those stellar spaces roll
The countless sparks and whorls of soul:
My constellation of the brain.

These bones are calm and beautiful;
The flesh, like water, strains and clears
To show the face my future wears
Drowned at the bottom of its pool.

Then I am full of rage and bliss,
For in our naked bed I feel,
Mate of your panting mouth as well,
The deathshead lean toward your kiss;

And I am mad to have you here,
Now, Now, the instant shield of lust,
Deep in your flesh my flesh to thrust
Against a more tremendous fear.

For in a last analysis
The mind has finer rays that show
The woof of atoms, and below
The mathematical abyss;

The solid bone dissolving just
As this dim pulp about the bone;
And whirling in its void alone
Yearns a fine interstitial dust.

The ray that melts away my skin
Pales at that sub-atomic wave:
This shows my image in the grave,
But that the emptiness within

By which I know our contacts are
Delusive as a point of light
That froths against my shores of sight
Sent out from the remotest star,

So spent, that great sun's fiery head
Is scarcely visible; a ray
So ancient that it brings today
Word from a world already dead.

The Muse
To James McAuley, January 1945

She is Arachne. Instinct spins the net
Of her ferocious purpose in the night.
On her bared nerves the dew shakes bright and wet;
The angry goddess still with light
Tortures the web; for there the spider hangs
In loveliness no wisdom could invent
And conscious of the poison in her fangs.

She is Ariadne by the shore
Watching a black sail vanish on the sea,
While he, whose steps beyond the dreadful door
Were guided, and again set free,
The loutish prince forgets the path he trod;
And she, though she remembers, will consent
Soon to be tumbled by the drunken god.

She is Penelope. Nightlong at the loom
She must unravel the promise in her heart,
Subdue the monthly protest of the womb;
And still she knows, for all her art,
While its one poor design grows out of date,
The gods, who have all time, too late relent
And when her triumph comes, it comes too late.

The Dinner

Angels have dined with men, and when they do,
All that they touch and taste takes blessing too.
The world that lies within a night and day,
Ended with evening, all things pass away,
And, a new heaven and a new earth begun,
We meet as two, and touch and smile as one.
Then on my sleeve you lay your brilliant hand
And lead me to the lighted table land.

All things expect you: walls and ceiling swim
In mellower light; the chairs stand straight and trim;
The tables dressed with snow behold you come;
The mouth of every crystal glass is dumb;
The knives and forks in silver order shine
And grace descends upon the food and wine.

Delicate, young and cradled in delight,
You take your seat and bare your teeth to bite –
What is my courage then to suffer this
Miracle of your metamorphosis!
For in that instant I behold the jaws
Of the most terrible of carnivores
Tear at its prey; the ravening human packs
Pull down their terrified victim in its tracks;
The wit, the charm, the grace, the pride of life
Adore the bloody edges of a knife!
The nakedness I had my arms about
Was gorged in death – I see the cayman's snout
Snap the deer's nostrils as they touch the flood;
The tiger's hairy muzzle sweet with blood;
The condor, flapping from the rocky peak,
Light on the carrion, plunge his grisly beak
Into the rotting porridge; through the dark
Slides the lithe, cold torpedo of the shark.
The air, the jungle, the salt, cannibal sea
Hold no more ruthless beast of prey than she.
For her the ox falls snoring in his blood;
The lamb is butchered for her daily food;
Her exquisite mouth, that smiles and tastes the wine,
Has killed by proxy a whole herd of swine –

Her exquisite mouth! As men, when at the worst,
Envy past ills, a vision succeeds the first
For which how gladly would I take again
That vision of the bloody mouths of men!
Now from the ancient past are conjured crude
Terrors of the black cave and the blind wood:
There sits the giant at his monstrous board,
The giantess, massive as her shaggy lord,

Squats at the spit and bastes the sizzling meat,
Dresses the trencher, serves and takes her seat,
And, leaning on the plank her full, warm breasts,
Looks in his face and smiles. He takes and tests
His six-foot knife – the little ribs spring wide;
He cuts the liver steaming from its side.
Talking in deep, soft, grumbling undertones
They gnaw and crack and suck the marrowy bones.
The titbits and choice meats they pluck and press
Each on the other, with grave tenderness,
And touch and laugh; their strange, fierce features move
With the delight and confidence of love.
I watch their loves, I see their human feast
With the doomed comprehension of the beast;
I feel the sweat creep through my bristling hair;
Hollow with rage and fear, I crouch and stare,
And hear their great jaws strip and crush and chew,
And know the flesh they rend and tear is you.

The House of God

Morning service! parson preaches;
People all confess their sins;
God's domesticated creatures
Twine and rub against his shins;

Tails erect and whiskers pricking,
Sleeking down their Sunday fur,
Though demure, alive and kicking,
All in unison they purr:

Lord we praise Thee; hear us Master!
Feed and comfort, stroke and bless!
And not too severely cast a
Glance upon our trespasses:

"Yesterday we were not able
To resist that piece of fish
Left upon the kitchen table
While You went to fetch the dish;

"Twice this week a scrap with Rover;
Once, at least, we missed a rat;
And we *do* regret, Jehovah,
Having kittens in Your hat!

"Sexual noises in the garden,
Smelly patches in the hall –
Hear us, Lord, absolve and pardon;
We are human after all!"

Home at last from work in Heaven,
This is all the rest God gets;
Gladly for one day in seven
He relaxes with His pets.

Looking down He smiles and ponders,
Thinks of something extra nice:
From His beard, O Joy, O wonders!
Falls a shower of little mice.

The Elegy
Variations on a theme of the Seventeenth Century

Madam, no more! The time has come to eat.
The spirit of man is nourished, too, with meat.
Those heroes and the warriors of old –
Feasting between their battles made them bold.
When Venus in the west hung out her lamp,
The rattling sons of Mars marched home to camp;
And while around the fires their wounds were dressed,
And tale was matched with tale, and jest with jest,
Flagons of wine and oxen roasted whole
Refreshed their bodies and restored the soul.

Come, leave the bed; put on your dress; efface
Awhile this dazzling armoury of grace!
Flushed and rejoicing from the well-fought fight
Now day lies panting in the arms of night;
The first dews tremble on the darkening field;
Put up your naked weapons, the bright shield
Of triumph glinting to the early stars;
Call our troops home with trumpets from their wars;
And, as wise generals, let them rest and dine
And celebrate our truce with meat and wine.
See, the meek table on our service waits;
The devil in crystal winks beside our plates;
These veterans of love's war we shall repay
And crown with feasts the glories of the day.

Think no disgrace, if now they play a part
Less worthy of the soldiers of the heart.
Though these we led were granted, even as we,
Their moment's draught of immortality,
We do but snatch our instant on the height,
And in the valleys still live out the night.
Yet they surrender nothing which is theirs.
Nature is frugal in her ministers;
Each to some humbler office must return,
And so must we. Then grudge it not, but learn
In this the noble irony of kind:
These fierce, quick hands that rove and clasp must find
Other employment now with knife and fork;
Our mouths that groaned with joy, now eat and talk;
These chief commanders, too, without debate,
Sink to the lowliest service of the state.
Only our eyes observe no armistice;
Sparkling with love's perpetual surprise,
Their bright vedettes keep watch from hill to hill,
And, when they meet, renew the combat still.
And yet to view you would I linger on:
This is the rarest moment, soonest gone.
While now the marching stars invest the sky
And the wide lands beneath surrendered lie,
Their streams and forests, parks and fields and farms,

Like this rich empire tranquil in my arms,
Seem lovelier in the last withdrawing light
And, as they vanish, most enchant the sight.
Still let me watch those countries as they fade,
And all their lucid contours sink in shade;
The mounting thighs, the line of flank and breast
Yet harbour a clear splendour from the west,
Though twilight draws into its shadowy reign
This breathing valley and that glimmering plain,
Still let my warrior heart with fresh delight
Rove and reflect: "Here, here began the fight;
Between those gentle hills I paused to rest,
And on this vale the kiss of triumph pressed;
There, full encircled by the frantic foe,
I rode between the lilies and the snow;
And, in this copse that parts the dark and shine,
Plundered the treasures of the hidden mine;
Down those long slopes in slow retreat I drew;
And here renewed the charge; and here, anew
Met stroke with stroke and touched, at the last breath,
The unimagined ecstasy of death."

Full darkness! Time enough the lamps were lit.
Let us to dinner, Madam; wine and wit
Must have their hour, even as love and war,
And what's to come revives what went before.
Come now, for see the Captain of my lust,
He had so stoutly fought and stiffly thrust,
Fallen, diminished on the field he lies;
Cover his face, he dreams in paradise.
We, while he sleeps, shall dine; and, when that's done,
Drink to his resurrection later on.

The Martyrdom of St Teresa

There was a sudden croon of lilies
Drifting like music through the shop;
The bright knives flashed with heavenly malice,
The choppers lay in wait to chop;

And Jesus with his crown of briar
Worn like a little hat in *Vogue*
Picked up her soul of ruby fire
And popped it in his shopping bag.

She was so small a saint, a holy
Titbit upon the butcher's block –
Death chose the cuts with care and slowly
Put on his apron, eyed the clock

And sitting down serenely waited
Beside the plump brown carcass there,
Which kings had feared and the popes hated,
Which had known neither hate nor fear;

While through all Spain mysterious thunder
Woke cannibal longings in the blood,
Inviting man to put asunder
The flesh that had been joined with God.

The little nuns of her foundation
Arrived on foot, by mule or cart,
Each filled with meek determination
To have an elbow, or the heart.

Death with a smile expertly slices
A rib for one, for one the knee,
Cuts back a breast, cuts deeper, prises
Out the raw heart for all to see;

In Sister Philomena's basket
Safe for St Joseph's lies an arm;
The saw shrills on a bone, the brisket
Becomes a miracle working charm;

At five to six Death drops his cleaver:
The sunset, as the crowd goes home,
Pours down on every true believer
The mystic blood of martyrdom.

The Pleasure of Princes

What pleasures have great princes? These: to know
Themselves reputed mad with pride or power;
To speak few words – few words and short bring low
This ancient house, that city with flame devour;

To make old men, their father's enemies,
Drunk on the vintage of the former age;
To have great painters show their mistresses
Naked to the succeeding time; engage

The cunning of able, treacherous ministers
To serve, despite themselves, the cause they hate,
And leave a prosperous kingdom to their heirs
Nursed by the caterpillars of the state;

To keep their spies in good men's hearts; to read
The malice of the wise, and act betimes;
To hear the Grand Remonstrances of greed,
Led by the pure; cheat justice of her crimes;

To beget worthless sons and, being old,
By starlight climb the battlements, and while
The pacing sentry hugs himself for cold,
Keep vigil like a lover, muse and smile,

And think, to see from the grim castle steep
The midnight city below rejoice and shine:
"There my great demon grumbles in his sleep
And dreams of his destruction, and of mine."

36

The Trophy

This the builder cannot guess,
Nor the lover's utmost skill:
In the instant of success
Suddenly the heart stands still;

Suddenly a shadow falls
On the builder's finished plan,
And the cry of love appals
All the energies of man.

What dire symbol of the heart
Comes, then, from its ancient tomb?
Image both of love and art,
See the Roman soldier come!

What great captain breaks his rest
All the annals cannot tell –
Stone lies blank upon his breast;
Bitter laurel shades him well –

What great captain's rigid will
Checked in flight his rabble host,
Roused them, drove them, cheered them still,
Though they knew the battle lost;

And, when the campaign was won
By the single force of pride,
Heard the ghost within him groan,
Fell upon his sword and died.

The Death of the Bird

For every bird there is this last migration:
Once more the cooling year kindles her heart;
With a warm passage to the summer station
Love pricks the course in lights across the chart.

Year after year a speck on the map, divided
By a whole hemisphere, summons her to come;
Season after season, sure and safely guided,
Going away she is also coming home.

And being home, memory becomes a passion
With which she feeds her brood and straws her nest,
Aware of ghosts that haunt the heart's possession
And exiled love mourning within the breast.

The sands are green with a mirage of valleys;
The palm-tree casts a shadow not its own;
Down the long architrave of temple or palace
Blows a cool air from moorland scarps of stone.

And day by day the whisper of love grows stronger;
That delicate voice, more urgent with despair,
Custom and fear constraining her no longer,
Drives her at last on the waste leagues of air.

A vanishing speck in those inane dominions,
Single and frail, uncertain of her place,
Alone in the bright host of her companions,
Lost in the blue unfriendliness of space,

She feels it close now, the appointed season:
The invisible thread is broken as she flies;
Suddenly, without warning, without reason,
The guiding spark of instinct winks and dies.

Try as she will, the trackless world delivers
No way, the wilderness of light no sign,
The immense and complex map of hills and rivers
Mocks her small wisdom with its vast design.

And darkness rises from the eastern valleys,
And the winds buffet her with their hungry breath,
And the great earth, with neither grief nor malice,
Receives the tiny burden of her death.

William Butler Yeats

To have found at last that noble, candid speech
In which all things worth saying may be said,
Which, whether the mind asks, or the heart bids, to each
Affords its daily bread;

To have been afraid neither of lust nor hate,
To have shown the dance, and when the dancer ceased,
The bloody head of prophecy on a plate
Borne in at Herod's feast;

To have loved the bitter, lucid mind of Swift,
Bred passion against the times, made wisdom strong;
To have sweetened with your pride's instinctive gift
The brutal mouth of song;

To have shared with Blake uncompromising scorn
For art grown smug and clever, shown your age
The virgin leading home the unicorn
And loosed his sacred rage –

But more than all, when from my arms she went
That blessed my body all night, naked and near,
And all was done, and order and content
Closed the Platonic Year,

Was it *not* chance alone that made us look
Into the glass of the Great Memory
And know the eternal moments, in your book,
That we had grown to be?

The Judgement

Last Friday when the sun had set,
Under the stars the world was quiet.
I dreamed our Grand Assize was met,
And a great judge was there to try it.

39

I dreamed the bitter choice was past
That kept our lives so long asunder;
And in my arms I held you fast,
Until that summons broke in thunder.

It filled the world and shook the sky,
Crying our names through all creation,
And doomed our guilty hearts to die,
And after death proclaimed damnation.

A voice of warning and lament
For grace and mercy vainly shown us.
And naked from our bed we went,
The first fresh dews of sleep upon us.

And, as towards judgement, you and I
In the cool darkness walked together,
I felt the softness of your thigh
That brushed mine like a night-bird's feather;

I felt the hapless grief that rose,
And found your hand, and drew you nearer.
"Dear heart," you said and held me close,
"I weep for joy and not for terror;

"For joy that in your arms I lay
At last, nor cared that all men knew it;
And Heaven cannot take away
That bliss, nor Hell itself undo it."

Then once again the voice of dread
Called our two names in solemn warning –
And in my solitary bed
I woke to find the cold day dawning

Remembering, in helpless woe,
That love our bitter choice had ended,
The doom we spoke so long ago
That no damnation now could mend it.

Lot and His Daughters

I

The ruddy fire-glow, like her sister's eyes,
Flickered on her bare breasts and licked along
The ripeness of her savage flanks; a tongue
Of darkness curled between her restless thighs.

Black as the Syrian night, on her young head
Clustered the tendrils of their ancient vine;
The cave gaped with its drunken mouth; the wine
Babbled, unceasing, from the old man's bed:

"I have two daughters...let them serve your need
...virgins...but these, my guests...you understand" –
She crept in and lay down. Her Promised Land
Lay waiting for the sower with his seed.

She felt him stir; she felt herself embraced;
The tough old arms bit hard on loin and breast;
The great beard smothered her. She was possessed.
A lioness roared abruptly in the waste.

But Lot's grim heart was far away. Beside
The Jordan stream, in other days, he stood
And kept the great beast, raging, from her brood,
And drove his javelin through her tawny hide.

II

The sun above the hills raged in the height.
Within Lot's cave, his vine-stock's living screen
Filtered the noon-day glare to a dim green
And hung the fat grapes bunched against the light.

The rascal patriarch, the bad old man,
Naked and rollicking on his heap of straw,
Scratching his hairy cods – one drunken paw
Spilled the red liquor from its silver can.

41

His beard, white as a blossoming branch, gaped wide;
Out flew a laugh: "By God, the wine is out!
More wine!"
        The cavern rumbled to his shout.
Brown fingers pushed the leafy screen aside.

And, padding broadly with their barefoot tread,
Calm-eyed, big-bellied, purposeful and slow,
Lot's delicate daughters, in the bloom and glow
Of their fulfilment stood beside his bed.

Crafty from fear, reckless with joy and greed,
The old man held them in his crapulous eye:
Mountains of promise bulging in his sky;
Ark of his race; God's covenant to his seed.

They stooped to take his cup, tilted and poured;
The must rose mantling to the glittering rim;
And, as the heart of Lot grew bold in him,
It boasted and exulted in the Lord.

"The one Just Man from Sodom saved alive!
Did not His finger point me to this cave?
Behold His hand once more stretched out to save!
For Jahweh too is just. My seed shall thrive.

"Shall not the Judge of all the earth do right?
Why did his angels take me by the hand?
My tribe shall yet be numbered with the sand
Upon the shore and with the stars of night.

"With me it shall be as with Abraham.
Dark are His ways, but sure and swift to bless –
How should my ewes breed in the wilderness?
And lo, the Lord himself provides a ram!"

But Lot's resourceful daughters, side by side,
Smiled back, inscrutable, patient and content;
Their slender bodies, ripe and eloqent,
Swayed like the standing corn at harvest-tide.

And, conscious of what trouble stirred below
His words and flickered in his shrewd old eyes,
They placed the cup that kept their father wise
In that best wisdom, which is not to know.

The Lamp and the Jar

You are that vessel full of holy oil:
Wisdom, unstirring in its liquid sleep,
Hoarded and cool, lucid and golden green,
Fills the pure flanks of the containing stone;
Here darkness mellows what the sunlit soil
To purposes unknown, for ends unseen,
Produced, and labour of unnumbered men.
All the unthinking earth with fret or toil
Reared, ripened, buried in the earth again,
Here lives, and living, waits: this source alone
Distils those fruitful tears the Muses weep.

And I, the lamp before the sacred ark,
The root of fire, the burning flower of light,
Draw from your loins this inexhaustible joy.
There the perpetual miracle of grace
Recurs, as, from its agony, the flame
Feeds the blind heart of the adoring dark;
And there the figures of our mystery,
The shapes of terror and inhuman woe,
Emerge and prophesy; there with the mark
Of blood upon his breast and on his brow,
An unknown king, with my transfigured face,
Bends your immortal body to his delight.

The Brides

Down the assembly line they roll and pass
Complete at last, a miracle of design;
Their chromium fenders, the unbreakable glass,
The fashionable curve, the air-flow line.

Grease to the elbows Mum and Dad enthuse,
Pocket their spanners and survey the bride;
Murmur: "A sweet job! All she needs is juice!
Built for a life-time – sleek as a fish. Inside

"He will find every comfort: the full set
Of gadgets; knobs that answer to the touch
For light or music; a place for his cigarette;
Room for his knees; a honey of a clutch."

Now slowly through the show-room's flattering glare
See her wheeled in to love, console, obey,
Shining and silent! Parson with a prayer
Blesses the number-plate, she rolls away

To write her numerals in his book of life;
And now, at last, stands on the open road,
Triumphant, perfect, every inch a wife,
While the corks pop, the flash-light bulbs explode.

Her heavenly bowser-boy assumes his seat;
She prints the soft dust with her brand-new treads,
Swings towards the future, purring with a sweet
Concatenation of the poppet heads.

Imperial Adam

Imperial Adam, naked in the dew,
Felt his brown flanks and found the rib was gone.
Puzzled he turned and saw where, two and two,
The might spoor of Jahweh marked the lawn.

44

Then he remembered through mysterious sleep
The surgeon fingers probing at the bone,
The voice so far away, so rich and deep:
"It is not good for him to live alone."

Turning once more he found Man's counterpart
In tender parody breathing at his side.
He knew her at first sight, he knew by heart
Her allegory of sense unsatisfied.

The pawpaw drooped its golden breasts above
Less generous than the honey of her flesh;
The innocent sunlight showed the place of love;
The dew on its dark hairs winked crisp and fresh.

This plump gourd severed from his virile root,
She promised on the turf of Paradise
Delicious pulp of the forbidden fruit;
Sly as the snake she loosed her sinuous thighs,

And waking, smiled up at him from the grass;
Her breasts rose softly and he heard her sigh –
From all the beasts whose pleasant task it was
In Eden to increase and multiply

Adam had learned the jolly deed of kind:
He took her in his arms and there and then,
Like the clean beasts, embracing from behind,
Began in joy to found the breed of men.

Then from the spurt of seed within her broke
Her terrible and triumphant female cry,
Split upward by the sexual lightning stroke.
It was the beasts now who stood watching by:

The gravid elephant, the calving hind,
The breeding bitch, the she-ape big with young
Were the first gentle midwives of mankind;
The teeming lioness rasped her with her tongue;

The proud vicuña nuzzled her as she slept
Lax on the grass; and Adam watching too
Saw how her dumb breasts at their ripening wept,
The great pod of her belly swelled and grew,

And saw its water break, and saw, in fear,
Its quaking muscles in the act of birth,
Between her legs a pigmy face appear,
And the first murderer lay upon the earth.

The Return of Persephone

Gliding through that dead air, he made no sound;
Wing-shod and deft, dropped almost at her feet,
And searched the ghostly regiments, and found
The living eyes, the tremor of breath, the beat
Of blood in all that bodiless underground.

She left her majesty, she loosed the zone
Of darkness and put by the rod of dread.
Standing, she turned her back upon the throne
Where, well she knew, the Ruler of the Dead,
Lord of her body and being, sat like stone;

Stared with his ravenous eyes to see her shake
The midnight drifting from her loosened hair,
The girl once more in all her actions wake,
The blush of colour in her cheeks appear
Lost with her flowers that day beside the lake.

The summer flowers scattering, the shout,
The black manes plunging down to the black pit –
Memory or dream? She stood awhile in doubt,
Then touched the Traveller God's brown arm and met
His cool bright glance and heard his words ring out:

"Queen of the Dead and Mistress of the Year!"
– His voice was the ripe ripple of the corn,
The touch of dew, the rush of morning air –
"Remember now the world where you were born;
The month of your return at last is here."

And still she did not speak but turned again
Looking for answer, for anger, for command:
The eyes of Dis were shut upon their pain;
Calm as his marble brow, the marble hand
Slept on his knee. Insuperable disdain

Foreknowing all bounds of passion, of power, of art,
Mastered but could not mask his deep despair.
Even as she turned with Hermes to depart,
Looking her last on her grim ravisher
For the first time she loved him from her heart.

The Twenty-Second Sonnet of Louise Labé

O happy, fortunate, shining Sun, to see
Your friend and mistress always face to face;
And happy Moon: Endymion's embrace
Waits you as honey stored awaits the bee!

Mars beholds Venus, Mercury on the wing
Glides through each heaven, each land, with even pace;
And Jove looks down and views in many a place
The lustier times and trophies of his spring.

See how the harmony that reigns on high
Links with its force these bodies of the sky,
But had they not their loves, in toil and pain
They would break frame and order, and disperse
With random steps through a wrecked universe
Like me to search, and search, like me, in vain.

Meditation on a Bone

A piece of bone, found at Trondhjem in 1901, with the following
runic inscription (about A.D. 1050) cut on it:
*I loved her as a maiden; I will not trouble Erlend's detestable wife;
better she should be a widow.*

Words scored upon a bone,
Scratched in despair or rage –
Nine hundred years have gone;
Now, in another age,
They burn with passion on
A scholar's tranquil page.

The scholar takes his pen
And turns the bone about,
And writes those words again.
Once more they seethe and shout,
And through a human brain
Undying hate rings out.

"I loved her when a maid;
I loathe and love the wife
That warms another's bed:
Let him beware his life!"
The scholar's hand is stayed;
His pen becomes a knife

To grave in living bone
The fierce archaic cry.
He sits and reads his own
Dull sum of misery.
A thousand years have flown
Before that ink is dry.

And, in a foreign tongue,
A man, who is not he,
Reads and his heart is wrung
This ancient grief to see,
And thinks: When I am dung,
What bone shall speak for me?

Soledades of the Sun and the Moon
For P.K. Page

Now the year walks among the signs of heaven,
Swinging her large hips, smiling in all her motions,
Crosses with dancing steps the Milky Valley.
Round her the primal energies rejoice;
All the twelve metaphysical creatures and the seven
Swift spheres adore her vigour; the five oceans
   Look up and hear her voice
Ring through the ebony vault, where Ara Celi
Flames, and the choiring stars at their devotions
   With pure and jubilant noise
Praise and proclaim four seasons in her belly.

Four glittering worms, they sleep curled up inside her,
The unborn children of our isolation.
Solstice or song, in swift pursuit forever
We grieve in separate festivals of light.
What winged stallion, what immortal rider
Forks those wild flanks? What milk of generation
   Fills at a thrust the bright
Throat of the womb? By what supreme endeavour
Do the chaste Muses still take inspiration
   And tune the strings aright
By the god's bow that twangs to slay and sever?

Aimer of pestilence, Lucifer of healing,
Destroyer of the piping faun, Apollo!
Join these divided hearts. In single chorus
The raving sibyl and the lucid seer
Find words to the one music, each revealing
Light in the other's dark, dark in that shining, hollow
   Galactic hemisphere
Which spins the changeless images before us.
Sign after sign, the constellations follow,
   Mirrored across the year
Where Scorpio views her house of death in Taurus.

Where the Wise Archer hangs his glittering quiver
Each son of Leda greets a heavenly brother.
As country or sex or song or birth conspire
The hemispheres set their crystal walls between.
Narcissus in air, Narcissus in the river
Drown in an alien element, or smother
   The lives towards which they lean.
Yet, through the burning circles of desire,
Immortal spirits behold, each in the other:
   His pillar of flame serene,
She, the unknown somnambulist of her fire.

Cradles of earth receive the salamander
But once at most in any generation;
Once in an age a desert tribe surprises
The solitary bird, the burning tree;
Innocent of their state, the poets wander,
Seeking the kindred of their incarnation,
   Waste land and homeless sea.
Phosphor declining as Orion rises
May for a brief hour break his isolation,
   The dying Phoenix see
New Phoenix blazing in her nest of spices.

Only in space, not time, the pattern changes:
Over your land of memory, enchanted
Glides the Celestial Swan, and in your bitter
Darkness the She-Bear shambles round the Pole;
Anvils of summer, in mine, the iron ranges
Rise from its arid heart to see the haunted
   River of Light unroll
Towards Achernar, where Hermes, the transmitter
Of spirits, herald of men and gods, has granted
   Speech between soul and soul,
And each to each the Swan and Phoenix glitter.

The mortal hearts of poets first engender
The parleying of those immortal creatures;
Then from their interchange create unending
Orbits of song and colloquies of light;
Sexes in their apocalyptic splendour
In mutual contemplation of their natures
    Transfigure or unite;
Descant and burden in diapason blending,
Urania dances, and the sacred gestures
    Become the words we write,
My lark arising or your dove descending.

For you the gods of song forgo their quarrel;
Panther and Wolf forget their former anger;
For you this ancient ceremony of greeting
Becomes a solemn apopemptic hymn.
Muses who twine the ivy with the laurel
In savage measures celebrate you, Stranger;
    For you the Maenads trim
Their torches and, in order due repeating
The stately ode, invoke you. Wanderer, Ranger,
    Beyond the utmost rim
Of waters, hear the voice of these entreating!

And, as the solitary bird of passage,
Loosing her heart across the wastes of ocean,
Sees round the cliffs of home the black tide crawling,
Accept the incantation of this verse;
Read its plain words; divine the secret message
By which the dance itself reveals a notion
    That moves our universe.
In the star rising or the lost leaf falling
The life of poetry, this enchanted motion,
    Perpetually recurs.
Take, then, this homage of our craft and calling!

Put on your figures of fable: with the chalice
From which the poets alone drink wisdom, healing
And joy that weds the thyrsus with the lyre,
Be Circe – or be my Queen of Sheba; come
Silent at nightfall to my silent palace
And read my heart, and rest; and when the wheeling
   Signs of the sky turn home,
I shall arise and show you in his byre
Among your milk-white dromedaries kneeling,
   Fierce in that lilied gloom,
My horn of gold, my unicorn of fire.

The Watcher

Can the tree that grows in grief
Rooted in its own despair
Crown its head with bud and leaf,
Blossom and enrich the air?

Can the bird that on the bough
Tries the ripeness of the fruit,
Taste the agony below,
Know the worm that cuts the root?

In a dream I saw my tree
Clothed in paradisal white,
Every branch in ecstasy
Spread its odours on the night;

Lovers walking two and two
Felt their own delight expressed,
And the bird that thither flew
Chose its branches for her nest;

Children in a laughing tide
Thronged it round to taste and see;
"See the shining fruit," they cried,
"See the happy, blossoming tree!"

You alone among them there
Came with your divining heart,
Breathed that still, enchanted air,
Felt your tears in anguish start,

And the passion of your woe
At the sweetness of the fruit
Watered all the ground below,
Touched and healed the wounded root.

Then the bird among the leaves
Checked its song in sad surmise;
Then the lover saw what grieves
In the depth of human eyes;

But the children at your side
Took your hands and laughed to see
"O the shining fruit," they cried,
"O the happy, happy tree!"

Man Friday
For John Pringle

Saved at long last through Him whose power to save
Kept from the walking, as the watery grave,
Crusoe returned to England and his kind,
Proof that an unimaginative mind
And sober industry and commonsense
May supplement the work of Providence.
He, no less providential, and no less
Inscrutably resolved to save and bless,

Eager to share his fortune with the weak
And faithful servants whom he taught to speak,
By all his years of exile undeterred,
Took into exile Friday and the bird.

The bird no doubt was well enough content.
She had her corn – what matter where she went?
Except when once a week he walked to church,
She had her master's shoulder as a perch,
She shared the notice of the crowds he drew,
Who praised her language and her plumage too,
And, like a rational female, could be gay
On admiration and three meals a day.

But Friday, the dark Caribbean man,
Picture his situation if you can:
The gentle savage, taught to speak and pray,
On England's Desert Island cast away;
No godlike Crusoe issuing from his cave
Comes with his thunderstick to slay and save;
Instead from caves of stone, as thick as trees,
More dreadful than ten thousand savages,
In their strange clothes and monstrous mats of hair,
The pale-eyed English swarm to joke and stare,
With endless questions round him crowd and press
Curious to see and touch his loneliness.
Unlike his master Crusoe long before
Crawling half-drowned upon the desolate shore,
Mere ingenuity useless in his need,
No wreck supplies him biscuit, nails and seed,
No fort to build, no call to bake, to brew,
Make pots and pipkins, cobble coat and shoe,
Gather his rice and milk his goats and rise
Daily to some absorbing enterprise.

And yet no less than Crusoe he must find
Some shelter for the solitary mind,
Some daily occupation, too, contrive
To warm his wits and keep the heart alive;
Protect among the cultured, if he can,

The "noble savage" and the "natural man".
As Crusoe made his clothes, so he no less
Must labour to invent his nakedness
And, lest their alien customs, without trace
Absorb him, tell the legends of his race
Each night aloud in the soft native tongue
That filled his world when, bare and brown and young,
His brown, bare mother held him at her breast,
Then say his English prayers and sink to rest.
And each day waking in his English sheets,
Hearing the wagons in the cobbled streets,
The morning bells, the clatter and cries of trade,
He must recall, within their palisade,
The sleeping cabins in the tropic dawn,
The rapt, leaf-breathing silence, and the yawn
Of naked children as they wake and drowse,
The women chattering round their fires, the prows
Of wet canoes nosing the still lagoon.
At each meal, handling alien fork or spoon,
Remember the spiced mess of yam and fish
And the brown fingers meeting in the dish,
Remember too those island feasts, the sweet
Blood frenzy and the taste of human meat.

Thus he stored memories against his need,
In vain! For still he found the past recede;
Try as he would, recall, relive, rehearse,
The cloudy images would still disperse,
Till, as in dreams, the island world he knew
Confounded the fantastic with the true,
While England, less unreal day by day,
The Cannibal Island, ate his past away.
But for the brooding eye, the swarthy skin,
That witnessed to the Natural Man within,
Year following year, by inches, as they ran,
Transformed the savage to an Englishman.
Brushed, barbered, hatted, trousered and baptized,
He looked, if not completely civilized,
What came increasingly to be the case:
An upper servant, conscious of his place,

Friendly but not familiar in address
And prompt to please without obsequiousness,
Adept to dress, to shave, to carve, to pour
And skilled to open or refuse the door,
To keep on terms with housekeeper and cook
But quell the maids and footmen with a look.
And now his master, thoughtful for his need,
Bought him a wife and gave him leave to breed.
A fine mulatto, once a lady's maid,
She thought herself superior to Trade,
And, reared on a Plantation, much too good
For a low native Indian from the wood.
Yet they contrived at last to rub along,
For he was strong and kind, and she was young,
And soon a father, then a family man,
Friday took root in England and began
To be well thought of in the little town,
And quoted in discussions at "The Crown",
Whether the Funds would fall, the French would treat,
Or the new ministry could hold its seat.
For though he seldom spoke, the rumour ran
The master had no secrets from his man,
And Crusoe's ventures prospered so, in short,
It was concluded he had friends at Court.

Yet, as the years of exile came and went,
Though first he grew resigned and then content,
Had you observed him close, you might surprise
A stranger looking through the servant's eyes.
Some colouring of speech, some glint of pride,
Not born of hope, for hope long since had died,
Not even desire, scarce memory at last,
Preserved that stubborn vestige of the past.

It happened once that man and master made
A trip together on affairs of trade;
A ship reported foundered in the Downs
Brought them to visit several seaport towns.
At one of these, Great Yarmouth or King's Lynn,
Their business done, they baited at an inn,

And in the night were haunted by the roar
Of a wild wind and tide against the shore.
Crusoe soon slept again, but Friday lay
Awake and listening till the dawn of day.
For the first time in all his exiled years,
The thunder of the ocean filled his ears.
And that tremendous voice so long unheard
Released and filled and drew him, till he stirred
And left the house and passed the town, to reach
At last the dunes and rocks and open beach;
Pale, bare and gleaming in the break of day
A sweep of new-washed sand around the bay,
And spindrift driving up the bluffs like smoke
As the long combers reared their crests and broke.
There in the sand beside him Friday saw
A single naked footprint on the shore.
His heart stood still, for as he stared, he knew
The foot that made it never had worn shoe
And at a glance, that no such walker could
Have been a man of European blood.
From such a footprint once he could describe
If not the owner's name, at least his tribe,
And tell his purpose as men read a face,
And still his skill sufficed to know the race,
For this was such a print as long ago
He too had made and taught his eyes to know.
There could be no mistake. Awhile he stood
Staring at that grey German Ocean's flood,
And suddenly he saw those shores again
Where Orinoco pours into the main,
And, stunned with an incredible surmise,
Heard in his native tongue once more the cries
Of spirits silent now for many a day
And all his years of exile fell away.

The sun was nearly to the height, before
Crusoe arrived hallooing at the shore,
Followed the footprints to the beach and found
The clothes and shoes and thought his servant drowned.

57

Much grieved he sought him up and down the bay,
But never guessed, when later in the day
They found the body drifting in the foam,
That Friday had been rescued and gone home.

A Bidding Grace

For what we are about to hear, Lord, Lord,
The dreadful judgement, the unguessed reprieve,
The brief, the battering, the jubilant chord
Of trumpets quickening this guilty dust
Which still would hide from what it shall receive,
Lord, make us thankful to be what we must.

For what we are now about to lose, reprove,
Assuage or comfort, Lord, this greedy flesh,
Still grieving, still rebellious, still in love,
Still prodigal of treasure still unspent.
Teach the blood weaving through its intricate mesh
The sigh, the solace, the silence of consent.

For what we are about to learn too late, too late
To save, though we repent with tears of blood:
The innocent ruined, the gentle taught to hate,
The love we made a means to its despair –
For all we have done, or did not when we could,
Redouble on us the evil these must bear.

For what we are about to say, urge, plead,
The specious argument, the lame excuse,
Prompt our contempt. When these archangels read
Our trivial balance, lest the shabby bill
Tempt to that abjectness which begs or sues,
Leave us one noble impulse: to be still.

For what we are about to act, the lust, the lie
That works unbidden, even now restrain
This reckless heart. Though doomed indeed to die,
Grant that we may, still trembling at the bar
Of Justice in the thud of fiery rain,
Acknowledge at last the truth of what we are.

In all we are about to receive, last, last,
Lord, help us bear our part with all men born;
And, after judgement given and sentence passed,
Even at this uttermost, measured in thy gaze,
Though in thy mercy, for the rest to mourn;
Though in thy wrath we stand, to stand and praise.

A Letter from Rome
For Dr Leonie Kramer

Rome, Rome! thou art no more
As thou has been!
Felicia Hemans

Hotel della Rotonda
ROME 1958

Man being transitory likes to act
As though he had all time to air his views.
Man being idle takes to rhyme. In fact
Journeying in the company of the Muse,
I'd just arrived at this hotel, unpacked,
Refurbished, washed my face and changed my shoes,
When in she came all smiles and said: "In Rome,
The thing to do is, write a letter home."

"My dear, good girl," I said, "do you forget a
Theme like this needs eagle wings to soar?
I might just rise to a familiar letter,
News, observations, gossip, nothing more.

Besides, it's all been done and done much better;
I've never tried that sort of thing before.
Australian poets, you recall, prefer
The packhorse and the slip-rail and the spur."

"High time they stopped it then," the Muse replied,
"I never liked that pioneering strain,
The tales of how those mountain horsemen ride –
Today they drive a truck or take a plane.
Australian poets, if they ever tried,
Might show at least a rudiment of brain,
And yours –" "All right," I answered with a grin,
"You've talked me into it, my dear; you win!"

So here I am in the Eternal City:
The Pantheon itself is just next door.
I might be wise, I might at least be witty
Where bards have been so eloquent before.
Some found her splendid, others thought her pretty,
Some said she was the Babylonian Whore;
But each was vocal, *vehemens et tremens*,
From Roman Virgil down to Mrs Hemans.

Yet travelling poets, even at the best,
Are apt to turn out bores or something worse;
Even *Childe Harold*, it must be confessed,
Is sometimes merely Baedeker in verse;
And for a new antipodean guest
Rome, as a subject, daunts if not deters;
But I, since she demands my tribute, can
At least contrive to write some lines that scan.

And since I'm launched now in *ottava rima*,
– For easy-going verse it's just the thing –
I shan't attempt the high poetic theme or
Pitch my note to make the welkin ring.
That *"Roma non è più come era prima"*
Which Byron heard the Roman workmen sing
Gives scope to write on anything at all
Since Romulus and Remus built their wall.

I might compile a *Muses' Guide to Rome*,
Describing all the sights and trips and treats,
Label the cells that cram the honeycomb,
The haunts of poets and their favourite streets,
The gate where Ovid lingered leaving home,
The oak of Tasso and the tomb of Keats,
The booth where Horace bought Falernian wine,
The restaurant where Goethe used to dine.

I have just dined myself extremely well
And drunk much wine, though not Falernian.
I might, if I were Goethe, who can tell,
Compose a new *West-Oestliche Diwan*,
Like Mrs Browning I might raise from hell
A Vision of the Poets, man by man,
And show you who was who, and what was what;
But something warns me I had better not.

A man, of course, should know his limitations
And, only if he has one, trust his star.
But poets ought to risk their reputations
To find out what those limitations are;
And modern poets put me out of patience
Wanting the grace, or guts, to aim too far.
So in this instance I shall *not* proceed
To emulate the Venerable Bede.

Just think of Bede the Tourist! – I, you see, am
Not drunk, but just a little "flown with wine" –
Bede came to Rome and offered his Te Deum,
Fresh from a land as barbarous as mine,
Made one remark about the Colosseum
And plodded back to Jarrow-on-the-Tyne.
And think of Bede the Poet, satisfied
To leave *one* poem, composed the day he died!

But lacking Bede's restraint, I must beware
In Rome the pilgrim's more besetting sin,
Which made poor Mistress Kempe so hard to bear,
God's holy howler-monkey from King's Lynn,

Too much engrossed in Margery Kempe to spare
A page to the great city she was in,
For here I am with eighty lines set down
About myself and eight about the town.

So to my theme – and if I should digress,
As possibly I shall do by and by,
Skip as you please; most readers do, I guess,
Faced with the longer forms of poetry.
If I run on, one reason, I confess,
Is to employ the tongue and rest the eye:
Six weeks a tourist render me, alas,
As blind as Balaam, chattier than his ass.

The Tourist's fate though curiously reversed
Is that of Tantalus who watched a feast
Devoured by famine, who, consumed by thirst
Saw the cool waters rising to his breast.
The tourist has to cram until he burst
Or gulp until he vomit like a beast;
But either way the case is much the same;
The arrows of desire miss their aim.

Six weeks in Italy! He has to grapple
With all the culture that there is to see
In baptistery, temple, church or chapel,
Museum, mausoleum, gallery.
Adam was cursed for eating that one apple,
But had he finished the whole fatal tree
He might have found that gorging Good and Evil
Led less to Sin and Death than mere upheaval.

If asked to sink too fast too many bumpers,
No matter how felicitous the wine,
The mental belly will begin a rumpus
No matter though the matter is divine.
There is an end to what the eye can compass
Of perfect colour and superb design,
And whether art be sacred or profane,
To look too often is to look in vain.

Day after day, with guide-book at the ready,
I've stormed the galleries from hall to hall,
Where headless muse or mutilated lady
Are flanked by god unsexed or Dying Gaul.
Checking my members every night in bed, I
Have groaned, I must admit, as I recall
That on the morrow waits for me a fresh
Mountain of marble chiselled into flesh.

I've contemplated all the types of Venus
Which win the heart or take the soul by storm,
The modest fig-leaf and the shameless penis
In every proper or improper form,
Until the individual in the genus
Is lost and all exceptions in the norm,
And fair and foul and quaint and crass and crude
Dissolve in one vast cliché of the Nude.

I've seen enough Nativities to fluster
The whole collective Midwives' Fellowship,
More angels than scholastic wits could thrust a
Pin between, or count upon the tip,
More Virgins than St Ursula could muster
To chaperon that fatal one-way trip,
And Holy Families and Annunciations
By tribes and hordes and multitudes and nations.

I've viewed the pitch of human ingenuity
Record in bronze, in marble and in paint
New schemes and still new schemes in perpetuity
For martyrdoms – and some extremely quaint –
New ways to grill St Lawrence, if to do it he
Were forced to spatchcock that devoted saint,
New ways to stick Sebastian full of arrows
And scarify St What's-his-name with harrows.

Augustine possibly was optimistic
About the rout and ruin of pagan gods;
The City of God, triumphant book, was his stick,
The City of Rome had always other rods,

63

And Christian savages, no less sadistic
Than those who at the Circus had laid odds
Upon the lion and against the martyr,
Now took their pleasures in another quarter.

I grant the butchery of the arena
Was finished and the bad old days were done;
But brothers of the wolf and the hyena
Could still contrive to have their grisly fun;
Where painter vied with painter to give keener
Edge to the axe, make bloodier rivers run,
It gave a thrill as brutal, though vicarious,
To lop Eulalia or chop Januarius.

Yet saint or sadist, each could gaze his fill,
Or if unfilled come back another day.
Before a masterpiece the mind could still
Take time to learn, to ponder or to pray.
The modern tourist pays a job-lot bill,
Takes one quick look and then is whisked away:
"Next we see Titian's famous – Ah, too late!
Alas, messieurs, mesdames, our bus won't wait."

The Muses have no schedules, they are free,
But foreign travel, once a private venture
At best, is now a major industry
Where dividend and bonus and debenture
Compete with wisdom, love and piety.
Change them for comfort, uplift, tame adventure
And those who put a girdle round the earth
Will guarantee we get our money's worth.

The pilgrims of the age of faith bareshod
Tramped across Europe, singing by the way;
Innkeepers, robbers on the road they trod
Might wait and make of them their natural prey,
And Rome once reached, the ministers of God
For each act of devotion make them pay;
But no one sold them "culture" on the side
Or made them beggars to his Barmecide.

Romantic Felicaja! He was sure
His country had her scenery to thank
For all invasions, Lombard, Goth and Moor,
German and Spaniard, Saracen and Frank;
"The fatal gift of beauty", not the lure
Of rape, the simple urge to rob a bank,
Or what impels a Mohawk to take scalps,
Had led them up her coasts or through the Alps.

It was quite other armies the reward
Of Beauty drew – it draws them to this day –
The travelling gentleman, the young milord,
Hell-bent on culture, curios, women, play,
Drank, diced and duelled, dug for statues, whored,
Bought pictures or sketched ruins, came away
At last complete, accomplished, finished fellows,
Formed by her courts or poxed by her bordellos.

And after the Grand Tour there came the Trip
Abroad, a much more middle-class affair:
Migratory bards recovering from the pip,
The family party, the adulterous pair,
The archaeologists in a chartered ship,
Lounged, ate *gelati*, swam or stopped to stare
At Ruskin sketching every stone in Venice
Or Browning in his braces playing tennis.

Well "culture" in the eighties, at a guess,
Did little harm. As far as one can see,
Seasons in Italy were more or less
A leisured picnic, a light-hearted spree.
That dogged transatlantic earnestness
From which no nation now on earth is free,
Had not yet turned its pleasure into solemn
Lectures on how to look at Trajan's column.

It soon came on, indeed was on the way,
As Henry James depicted it, for one.
In any picture-gallery today
Kulturgeschichte takes away the fun

65

Unless one joins a group and cares to stay
To watch the Herr Professor toss the bun
To teach us peasants, munching it with zeal,
Not only what to think but how to feel.

However lucid, well-informed, vivacious,
The lecturer's task is hopeless from the start:
Most ready-made emotions are fallacious,
And there's no ready-made response to art.
Tibetan prayer-wheels may be efficacious
Since those who twirl them know the prayers by heart,
But these are devotees whose utmost skill
Consists in knowing how to gulp the pill.

Of course it would be stupid out of measure
To laugh at those who know their need to learn.
For some, perhaps, who never had the leisure
Nor yet the chance before, this serves their turn.
A tale I heard last week with simple pleasure
In Florence dots the i's of my concern,
And illustrates to what absurd degree
Some people will proceed to cross a t.

That evening I had dinner with a man
Who has lived forty years in Italy,
Half English, more than half Italian
With all the latter's gift of irony;
And while we drank our wine my host began
To talk of Florence and her history,
Her life, her people, and to finish off he
Told me the following story over coffee:

"In Florence there is a well-known foundation,
Richly endowed from the United States,
Trimmed to the latest trends in education,
It 'finishes' young women graduates
And gives them poise and polish for the station
Their family's bank-balance indicates,
The sort of thing entitled, as a rule,
A Continental Summer Graduate School.

"Its aims are serious, its methods sound,
Its courses academically respectable,
Fine Arts for those who like to shop around,
Western Philosophy for the directable,
And Poetry from Poe to Ezra Pound,
With, just to stiffen subjects so delectable,
A weekly seminar, a monthly test,
And Love is on the course with all the rest.

"Of course it is not on their syllabus,
As best confined to individual choice;
But hints are dropped in sessions to discuss
How to attain maturity and poise
That, if arranged discreetly, without fuss,
Brief love-affairs with nice Italian boys
May well repay the trouble and expense
Since nothing broadens like experience.

"Italian boys are not, and never were,
Averse to girls when rich, well-dressed and pretty.
The summer school created quite a stir
Among the young Lotharios of the city;
The alleys throbbed with an expectant purr;
The streets were filled with amorous banditti.
The girls of Florence, it may be, were less
Well-pleased, but that is anybody's guess.

"But how to set about it? How to find
A lover? That's quite simple in a town
Where every girl gets pinched on the behind
In shops, trams, church, or walking up and down.
It's half an invitation, half a kind
Of compliment. If she should turn and frown
That's that; but if she smiles, he'll raise his hat
And ask her to take coffee, and that's that!

"Louise, though very beautiful, was what I'm
Inclined to call a serious girl at heart,
And, though endowed with an attractive bottom,
Thought pinching it no proper way to start;

And Alessandro was well-bred; if not I'm
Sure he knew just how to act the part.
He met her at a concert, did not pinch,
But said the *pizzicati* made him flinch.

"She smiled and said: 'How's that?' The ice was broken.
He ordered coffee. She did not refuse.
They talked on various topics which betoken
The parties each have cultivated views.
And, as they talked their eyes said things unspoken.
The world was all before them, where to choose.
He saw her home and on the doorstep they
Arranged to meet again the following day.

"Louise went in and calmly jotted down
Some notes on her emotional reactions,
Removed her make-up, donned her dressing gown
And nicely planned her conduct and her actions;
While Alessandro wandered through the town
Enraptured by her charms and her attractions.
His plans were just the usual well-bred
Young man's to get the girl to go to bed.

"To his surprise, and more to his chagrin,
She went to bed without the least demur.
Passion expects resistance, and to win
Without it, on his passion cast a slur.
He loved her voice, her eyes, her shape, her skin,
But found no answering response in her.
She loved him, not for love however fiery,
But for providing data for her diary.

"They went to bed; they took a trip to Pisa;
They 'did' the Pitti; and they went to bed;
She told him all about herself; to please her
He talked about Etruscan tombs; she read
Her diary to him and that day to ease a
Sense of strain they took a walk instead;
They walked, they talked, she reasoned and he swore,
But in the end they went to bed once more.

"And at the close of a divine semester
She annotated and revised her notes,
Wrote 'Field-Work' on the cover and repressed a
Less serious urge to label it: 'Wild Oats'.
She can't say Europe very much impressed her,
Though Sandro is a name on which she dotes.
She thinks that Kinsey overrates the male."
And here my host broke off his merry tale.

A Merry Tale? Boccaccio might have written:
"How Messer Sandro wooed a learnèd dame,
But found his labour lost, the biter bitten
And half a thesis cooked upon his flame."
Yet I am sad to see so many smitten
By the same view of art and much the same
Approach as this poor girl's who thought her fee
Made Love one more post-graduate degree.

But, talking of degrees, the Schedule Beaters
On any scale of nonsense touch the top.
Hung round with cameras, light-filters, meters,
Always on time and travelling till they drop,
They pause – a wife identifies St Peter's,
They never look at all, but make a stop,
Squint, fiddle, click and, happy, hurry back
To Bristol, Cincinnati or Toorak.

Watching these futile pilgrims in their legions
Who must get home to find where they have been,
I find myself who owe them no allegiance,
Caught in a farce as senseless as obscene,
Asking what brings me here from those dim regions
Where Dante planted Hell's Back Door, and Dean
Swift his microcosm of civilization?
The facts fell short of their imagination,

For I am no infernal refugee
And reach a normal height of five foot nine.
Yet there is something strange, I would agree,
In those dumb continents below the Line.

The roots are European but the tree
Grows to a different pattern and design;
Where the fruit gets its flavour I'm not sure,
From native soil or overseas manure.

And this uncertainty is in our bones.
Others may think us smug or insular;
The voice perhaps is brash, its undertones
Declare in us a doubt of what we are.
When the divided ghost within us groans
It must return to find its avatar.
Though this puts things too solemnly, of course,
Yet here am I returning to the source.

That source is Italy, and hers is Rome,
The *fons et origo* of Western Man;
Athens perhaps begot, Rome was the womb;
Here the great venture of the heart began.
Here, simply with a sense of coming home
I have returned with no explicit plan
Beyond a child's uncertain quest to find
Something once dear, long lost and left behind.

The clue lies not in art or history,
Relics or ruins that survive their prime.
The thing I came to find was lost in *me*,
Not in the Forum's dust, the Tiber's slime.
The act which resurrects is just to be
Patient before these witnesses of time.
The graves may open and their dead appear,
But mine is the sepulchral voice I hear.

The efficacy of place, like that of prayer,
Lies in no overt effort of the will;
To keep the mind unquesting but aware,
The heart unmoving but responsive still
Opens the way to forces which prepare
Answers whose questions lie beyond our skill.
And this, I know, is what I have in view,
As other poets, I think, have felt it too.

And one especially is in my mind:
The limping man, the legend of his age.
Asking myself what *he* came here to find,
I've just re-read *Childe Harold's Pilgrimage*,
Which offers, almost equally combined,
The shrewd, the silly, the noble and the sage,
The stamp of genius and the touch of sham.
Well, I'm quite sure of one thing: that I am

Not like the Pilgrim of Eternity,
Revisiting the Muses' Campo Santo,
Not like his Harold – who indeed could be
Like Harold, and what man alive would want to?
Yet what moved Byron then, it seems to me,
To write his fourth, superb and final canto
Impels me too to write, although the scene
Is somewhat changed since eighteen seventeen.

What caused him to leave Venice? Well, he said
He'd like to take a trip and see the Pope,
Hinted he'd like a rest from too much bed
With a blonde charmer called the Antelope;
Writing to Murray for tooth-powder (red)
He said that Rome had drawn him with the hope
To make Constantinople's glories pale.
The poem, I think, tells quite another tale.

Unlike that desultory scenic stroll
Which robs his earlier cantos of their force,
This moves with sure direction and control
In towards the centre, back towards the source.
Its theme is destiny and Rome its goal;
And yet it does not stop with Rome; the course
Of history retraced, it moves at last
Into the savage, pre-historic past.

It ends with Nemi and the Golden Bough.
What instinct led him there? I like to think
What drew him then is what has drawn me now
To stand in time upon that timeless brink,

71

To sense there the renewal of a vow,
The mending of a lost primordial link.
These may be only fancies, yet I swear
I felt the presence of the numen there.

There's nothing now at Nemi to evoke
Sir James G. Frazer's memorable scene:
The sleepless victim-King, the sacred oak;
A market garden spreads its tidy green
Where stood Diana's grove; no voices spoke,
There were no omens; cloudless and serene
The sun beat harshly on the drowsing lake;
And yet I felt my senses wide awake,

Alert, expectant – as we scrambled down
The crater from the village to the shore
And strolled along its path, we were alone;
And picnicking among the rocks, I saw
No cause for these sensations. Yet I own
A tension grew upon me more and more.
What Byron felt as calm and cherished hate
For me was more like force, insistence, fate.

And under this impulsion from the place,
I seemed constrained before I came to drink,
To pour some wine upon the water's face,
Later, to strip and wade out from the brink.
Was it a plea for chrism or for grace?
An expiation? More than these, I think
I was possessed, and what possessed me there
Was Europe's oldest ritual of prayer.

But prayer to whom, for what? The Intervention
Did not reveal itself or what it meant.
The body simply prays without "intention".
The mind by the bare force of its assent,
That "higher, more extended comprehension",
Which Byron, writing after the event,
Felt necessary to explain brute fact,
Came by mere power of my consenting act.

Well, let it pass: I have no views about it;
Only I sensed some final frontier passed,
Some seed, long dormant, which has stirred and sprouted
Some link of understanding joined at last.
I may have been deluded, but I doubt it
Though where the series leads I can't forecast.
Laugh at these intimations if you will;
The days go by and they are with me still.

Meanwhile I walk and gaze. For all its size,
Rome is a city one can see on foot;
And that's the pace for such an enterprise.
Each morning we buy cheese and rolls and fruit
And stroll and stop to view whatever lies
Along a vague and ambulating route.
I miss a lot, of course, but what I see,
Because *I* found it, seems a part of *me*.

And as I walk I think of my own land
To which I must return when this trip's over.
She speaks a language that I understand
And wakes no love that "moves with the remover".
I fear this letter's getting out of hand
But there's a topic still I wish to cover
Which hangs upon a tale of Yin and Yang:
The *Abendland*'s reputed *Untergang*.

I'd like to say at once I've never much
Believed the prophets of impending doom,
The Spenglers, T.S. Eliots and such,
Guides to the Waste Lands and the Wrath to Come.
Perhaps I'm simply rather out of touch,
But I'm confirmed by what I sense in Rome.
She still is *urbs et orbis*, still the ground
Of generation and the roots are sound.

And yet, although the roots are sound enough,
A blight has touched the branches and the fruit.
The voice of wisdom falters and falls off
In aimless speculation and dispute.

73

The single, sure, tradition and the tough
Old faiths that fed and fostered it are mute,
And Italy from which the West arose
Falls prey to new but more barbarian foes.

Italia, O Italia, still in fetters,
Though risen at last, restored, united, free,
I too shall bring you from the world of letters
One more lament, though it is not for me
Perhaps to try to emulate my betters.
The tragic theme, the bough of prophecy
I leave to Dante, Ariosto, Byron,
Whose ages range from gold to brass to iron;

But mine's the age of plastics and alloys
Which bring combustion engines in their train
To fill with hideous and inhuman noise
All your once pleasant cities of the plain.
It is the curse of Hell that it destroys
Good of the intellect; the heat, the pain,
The darkness and the terror and the thirst
Are damnable, but not damnation's worst.

Though Dante found it crowded, hot and smelly,
His first impressions and most lasting were:
Accenti d'ira, orribili favelle,
The sounds of torment, discord and despair,
Screams from the tortured and the brute bass belly-
Chuckle of demons; yet if I might dare
Cap Dante I should give for "Hell let loose"
The din Italian motor-bikes produce.

It blinds the heart, it breaks the mind with menace,
Beats, batters, deafens, bruises, numbs, appals,
Ruins Rome's surge of life and blasts Ravenna's
Millennial slumber in her crumbling walls,
And pulverizes every town but Venice,
Which, God be praised, is saved by the canals.
Hearing it now, it seems to signify
The burden of the poet's anguished cry:

74

Servi Italia di dolore ostello!
As one by one your tyrants had their hour,
The arts could flourish still and though the fellow
Of lust and greed, the tree of man still flower.
But what can vie with this mechanic bellow,
The final, brutal voice of naked power,
As you, who spoke for Europe in your day,
Become its symbol for the mind's decay?

You spoke for Europe as you spoke for Man,
Taught him to pray, to probe, to dream, to dare;
In you his new entelechy began
Where now the yawp of Babel fills the air.
Who speaks for Europe now? The few who can
Know only the recourses of despair;
And none arise to find, renew, prolong
The harmonies of your enchanted song,

A song the Sibyl's murmur taught to grow
From age to age, until the centuries
Heard the high trumpets in their passion blow,
Now lost in mindless roar from the abyss.
The parables of history can show
Surely no sadder irony than this
Which brings that noble, intellectual voice
To drown in trivial and distracting noise.

The Coasts of Cerigo

Half of the land, conscious of love and grief,
Half of the sea, cold creatures of the foam,
Mermaids still haunt and sing among the coves.
Sailors, who catch them basking on the reef,
Say they make love like women, and that some
Will die if once deserted by their loves.

Off shore, in deeper water, where the swell
Smokes round their crests, the cliffs of coral plunge
Fathom by fathom to the ocean floor.
There, rooted to the ooze-bed, as they tell,
Strange sister to the polyp and the sponge,
To holothurian and madrepore,

The Labra wallows in her bath of time
And, drowned in timeless sleep, displays the full
Grace of a goddess risen from the wave.
Small scarlet-crabs with awkward gestures climb
Through the black seaweed drifting from her skull.
Her ladylegs gape darkly as a cave,

And through the coral clefts a gleam and gloom
Reveal the fronded arch, the pelvic gate;
Spotted and barred, the amorous fish swim in.
But in that hollow, mocking catacomb
Their love-songs echo and reverberate
A senseless clamour and a wordless din.

The love-trap closes on its gullible prey
Despite their sobs, despite their ecstasies.
Brilliant with tropic bands and stripes, they dart
Through a delicious juice which eats away
Their scales and soon dissolves their goggle eyes
And melts the milt-sac and the pulsing heart.

The divers on these coasts have cruel hands;
Their lives are hard; they do not make old bones;
The brutal masters send them down too deep.
But sometimes, as he combs the clefts and sands,
Among the oyster-beds and bearded stones
One comes upon the Labra fast asleep

And throws away his knife, his bag of pearl,
To take her in his arms and wrench her free.
Their bodies cling together as they rise
Spinning and drifting in the ocean swirl.
The seamen haul them in and stand to see
The exquisite, fabled creature as she dies.

But while in air they watch her choke and drown,
Enchanted by her beauty, they forget
The body of their comrade at her side,
From whose crushed lungs the bright blood oozing down
Jewel by ruby jewel from the wet
Deck drops and merges in the turquoise tide.

An Epistle: Edward Sackville to Venetia Digby

Ainsi, bruyante abeille, au retour du matin,
Je vais changer en miel les délices du thym.

First, last and always dearest, closest, best,
    Source of my travail and my rest,
The letter which I shall not send, I write
    To cheer my more than arctic night.
Sole day and all my summer in that year
    Of darkness, you were here,
Were here but yesterday, and still I go
    Rapt in its golden afterglow.
Caught in the webs of memory and desire,
    The cooling and the kindling fire,
Through all this house, from room to room I pace:
    Here at the stair we met; this place

You sat in; still I see you sitting there,
    As though some trace the printless air
Retained; a tremulous hush, as though you spoke,
    Enchants its silence; here your cloak
I held for you and here you looked farewell
    And went, but did not break the spell
By which I feel you here yet know you gone –
    So men who winking see the sun
And turn into the dark awhile descry
    His image on the dazzled eye.
But, like a tale, I tell it all again
    And gloss it with a scholar's pen,
For so Love, though he harvest all his store,

77

Gleans in bare fields to make it more.
Now like the garner ant when frosts begin,
   I have my harvest heaped within:
Abundance for my year to come, a feast
   Still cherished, still increased;
For all it spends from its ripe yesterday
   The heart shall copiously repay:
Words, glances, motions, all that I rehearse
   My joy transfigures – as great verse
From music may have a perfection lent
   More than the poet knew or meant;
And as the cunning craftsman can prolong
   Through cadences and shifts of song,
And make what was by nature beautiful,
   By art more dulcet, keen and full,
So from one day, one meeting, I prepare
   Music to last me out the year.

Yet I cannot recall it as I should;
   Too much surprised by joy I stood,
A child who finds his long expected treat,
   Coming, too sudden and too sweet –
Or greedily I gulped it like a beast
   And missed the true, the lasting taste.
"Poor beast," I say, "poor beast, indeed, who comes
   To be content with scraps and crumbs!
Poor heart, poor Lazarus, overjoyed to wait
   The scrapings of another's plate!"
For, though I could restore, vivid and strong,
   That late, pure, breathless trançe of song,
I know myself but a dumb listener, where
   I have sung bourdon to her air.

I that was rich, now at the treasury door
   May only glimpse that golden store
Piled in fantastic heaps; the jewelled shrine
   Worship, not touch, no longer mine;
At most, a starveling Tantalus, must see
   The shadow crop upon my tree
Slide through the hand and from my gaping lip

78

The mocking naiad glide and slip.
Or rather – for in similes of woe
    I lose my way – full well I know
The food was real: 'Twas I who could not eat
    The spirit's insubstantial meat,
Pleasure of angels, such as flesh and blood
    Taste not, though all may take their food.
I, who have held you in my human arms,
    Must gaze, as if on ghostly charms
Or on the painting of a mistress dead –
    Yet we both breathe and might to bed.

To bed! At the mere thought I feel arise
    That rebel in the flesh, who cries:
"It was no picture we saw yesterday,
    But she, in all the living play
Of light on restless body, limbs, hair, breast,
    Eyes, hands – what need to tell the rest?"
What need? But, ah, what sure recourse of joy!
    This nothing can or shall destroy,
Custom deny nor honour stand between,
    Nor your own change of heart demean.
He, whose you are, your husband and my friend
    – I do not grudge it, but commend –
Took when he took you hence, your picture too
    Lest I should keep some part in you.

What should I care, who had my gallery lined,
    Crowded with pictures of the mind?
What care for silk or lute string who possess
    The splendour of your nakedness,
The lily, the jet, the coral and the rose
    Varied in pleasure and repose?
Three years we lived as blessed angels do
    Who to each other show the true
Bareness of spirit, and only when they would
    Travel abroad wear flesh and blood.
So clothed we met the world: at set of sun,
    Our foolish, needful business done,
Home we would turn, eager to taste at even

Our native and our naked heaven.
So now by heart each single grace and all
    Their glowing postures I recall;
Absent, you come unbidden; present, you
    Walk naked to my naked view;
Dead, I could resurrect you from your dust;
    So exquisite, individual, just
The bare, bright flesh, I swear my eyes could tell
    You by throat, thighs or breast as well,
Or any least part almost, as your face.

    Alas, as courtiers out of place
Speak of the court, I boast, and dream the rest.
    In exile now and dispossessed,
I think of how we used so long ago,
    In that tremendous overthrow
Of our first worlds, when first we loved, first knew
    No world except these selves, this Two,
How we would laugh to see that Last World pass
    For real beyond our Wall of Glass;
And we untouched, untouchable, serene,
    Plighted within our magic screen,
Would pity those without, whose curious eyes
    Could see, could judge, could recognise,
Know with the mind, but coldly and in part,
    Not with the comprehending heart.
This was our game; and, with the growth of love,
    We said, these walls of glass remove;
We re-embody those shadows by our joy;
    The frontiers of desire deploy
Until our latitudes of grace extend
    Round the great globe and bend
Back on themselves, to end where we begin
    Love's wars that take the whole world in.
So little states, rich in great men and sound
    In arts and virtues, gather ground
And grow to empires mighty in their day.
    And we, we said, more blest than they,
Shall not decline as Persian kingdoms do
    Or those the Tartar overthrew.

Who lives outside our universal state?
And all within ourselves create.
Will angels fall twice, or the moon breed Turks?
Or dread we our own works? –
But even while the architects designed
The finials, their towers were mined.

He, your child-lover, twice reported dead,
Once false – but all was false – some said
He died at Pont-de-Cé, and some said not
But on rough alps his bones might rot –
For whom, though your heart grieved, it grieved as for
Childhood itself that comes no more,
Yet came, and not as ghosts come from the grave,
But as strong spirits come to save,
And claimed the love we buried long ago.
I watched it rise and live. I know,
Alas, I know, though I believed it not,
The spell he casts who breaks the knot;
And this you told me once and bade me learn
Even before his strange return.

Now it is I outside our Wall. I stand
And once a year may kiss that hand
Which once with my whole body of man made free –
O, my twice-lost Eurydice,
Twice must I make my journey down to Hell,
Twice its grim gods by prayer compel,
And twice, to win you only for a day,
The spirit's bitter reckoning pay,
Yet for my first default their just decree
Grants me to hear you now and see,
As deserts know peace, as barren waters calms,
Only forbidding me your arms.

Why, since my case is hopeless, do I still
Exacerbate this wrench of will
Against the force of reason, honour, rest
And all that is in manhood best?
Is not this second Orpheus worse than he

Who perished in his misery,
Torn by the drunken women in their chase
Among the echoing hills of Thrace?
To cherish and prolong the state I loathe
Am I not drunk or mad or both?

Not so! These torments mind and heart approve,
And are the sacrifice of love.
The soul, sitting apart, sees what I do,
Who win powers more than Orpheus knew,
Though he tamed tigers and enchanted trees
And broached the chthonic mysteries.
The gate beyond the gate that I found fast
Has opened to your touch at last.
Nothing is lost for those who pass this door:
They contemplate their world before,
And in the carcass of the lion come
Upon the unguessed honeycomb.

There are no words for this new happiness,
But such as fables may express.
Fabling I tell it then as best I can:
That pre-diluvian age of man
Most like had mighty poets even as ours,
Or grant them nobler themes and powers;
When Nature fashioned giants in the dew
Surely the morning Muses too
Created genius in an ampler mould
To celebrate her Age of Gold.
Yet think for lack of letters all was lost,
Think Homer's *Iliads* to our cost
Gone like those epics from before the Flood,
As, but for Cadmus, sure they would.

Books now preserve for us the boasts of time;
But what preserved them in the Prime?
Where did they live, those royal poems then,
But in the hearts and mouths of men?
Men of no special genius, talents, parts,
Patience their sole gift, all their arts

Memory, the nurse, not mother, of ancient songs.
    No seraph from God's fire with tongs
Took the live coal and laid it on their lips;
    And yet, until their last eclipse,
Age after age, those giant harmonies
    Lodged in such brains, as birds in trees.
The music of the spheres which no man's wit
    Conceives, once heard, he may transmit:
Love was that music and by love indeed
    We serve the greater nature's need.
As on the rough back of some stream in flood
    Whose current is by rocks withstood,
We see, in all that ruin and rush, endure
    A form miraculously pure,
A standing wave through which the waters race,
    Yet keeps its crystal shape and place,
So shapes and creatures of eternity
    We form or bear. Though more than we,
Their substance and their being we sustain
    Awhile, though they, not we, remain.
And still, while we have part in them, we can
    Surpass the single reach of man,
Put on strange powers and vision we knew not of –
    And thus it has been with my love:
Fresh modes of being, unguessed forms of bliss
    Have been, are mine: But more than this,
Our bodies, aching in their blind embrace,
    Once thought they touched the pitch of grace;
Made for that end alone, in their delight,
    They thought that single act and rite
Paid nature's debt and heaven's. Even so
    There was a thing they could not know:
Nature, who makes each member to one end,
    May give it powers which transcend
Its first and fruitful purpose. When she made
    The tongue for taste, who in the shade
Of summer vines, what speechless manlike brute,
    Biting sharp rind or sweeter fruit,
Could have conceived the improbable tale, the long
    Strange fable of the Speaking Tongue?

So Love, which Nature's craft at first designed
  For comfort and increase of kind,
Puts on another nature, grows to be
  The language of the mystery;
The heart resolves its chaos then, the soul
  Lucidly contemplates the whole
Just order of the random world; and through
  That dance she moves, and dances too.

The Double Looking Glass

See how she strips her lily for the sun:
The silk shrieks upward from her wading feet;
Down through the pool her wavering echoes run;
Candour with candour, shade and substance meet.

From where a wet meniscus rings the shin
The crisp air shivers up her glowing thighs,
Swells round a noble haunch and whispers in
The dimple of her belly....Surely eyes

Lurk in the laurels, where each leafy nest
Darts its quick bird-glance through the shifting screen.
....Yawn of the oxter, lift of liquid breast
Splinter their white shafts through our envious green

Where thuds this rage of double double hearts.
....My foolish fear refracts a foolish dream.
Here all things have imagined counterparts:
A dragon-fly dim-darting in the stream

Follows and watches with enormous eyes
His blue narcissus glitter in the air.
The flesh reverberates its own surprise
And startles at the act which makes it bare.

Laced with quick air and vibrant to the light,
Now my whole animal breathes and knows its place
In the great web of being, and its right;
The mind learns ease again, the heart finds grace.

I am as all things living. Man alone
Cowers from his world in clothes and cannot guess
How earth and water, branch and beast and stone
Speak to the naked in their nakedness.

....A silver rising of her arms, that share
Their pure and slender crescent with the pool
Plunders the braided treasure of her hair.
Loosed from their coils uncrowning falls the full

Cascade of tresses whispering down her flanks,
And idly now she wades a step, and stays
To watch the ripples widen to the banks
And lapse in mossy coves and rushy bays.

Look with what bliss of motion now she turns
And seats herself upon a sunny ledge,
Leans back, and drowsing dazzles, basking burns.
Susannah! ....what hiss, what rustle in the sedge;

What fierce susurrus shifts from bush to bush?
....Susannah! Susannah, Susannah! ....Foolish heart,
It was your own pulse lisping in a hush
So deep, I hear the water-beetle dart

And trace from bank to bank his skein of light,
So still the sibilance of a breaking bud
Speaks to the sense; the hairy bee in flight
Booms a brute chord of danger in my blood.

What danger though? The garden wall is high
And bolted and secure the garden door;
The bee, bold ravisher, will pass me by
And does not seek my honey for his store;

The speckled hawk in heaven, wheeling slow
Searches the tufts of grass for other prey;
Safe in their sunny banks the lilies grow,
Secure from rough hands for another day.

Alert and brisk, even the hurrying ant
Courses these breathing ranges unafraid.
The fig-tree, leaning with its leaves aslant
Touches me with broad hands of harmless shade.

And if the urgent pulses of the sun
Quicken my own with a voluptuous heat,
They warm me only as they warm the stone
Or the thin liquid paddling round my feet.

My garden holds me like its private dream,
A secret pleasure, guarded and apart.
Now as I lean above the pool I seem
The image of my image in its heart.

In that inverted world a scarlet fish
Drifts through the trees and swims into the sky,
So in the contemplative mind a wish
Drifts through its mirror of eternity.

A mirror for man's images of love
The nakedness of woman is a pool
In which her own desires mount and move,
Alien, solitary, purposeful.

Yet in this close were every leaf an eye,
In those green limbs the sap would mount as slow.
One with their life beneath an open sky,
I melt into the trance of time, I flow

Into the languid current of the day.
.... The sunlight sliding on a breathing flank
Fades and returns again in tranquil play;
Her eyelids close; she sleeps upon the bank.

Now, now to wreak upon her Promised Land
The vengeance of the dry branch on the bud.
Who shall be first upon her? Who shall stand
To watch the dragon sink its fangs in blood?

Her ripeness taunts the ignominy of age;
Seethes in old loins with hate and lust alike.
Now in the plenitude of shame and rage
The rod of chastisement is reared to strike.

And now to take her drowsing; now to fall
With wild-fire on the cities of the plain;
Susannah!.... Yet once more that hoarse faint call,
That rustle from the thicket comes again?

Ah, no! Some menace from the edge of sleep
Imposes its illusion on my ear.
Relax, return, Susannah; let the deep
Warm tide of noonday bear you; do not fear,

But float once more on that delicious stream.
Suppose some lover watches from the grove;
Suppose, only suppose, those glints, the gleam
Of eyes; the eyes of a young man in love.

Shall I prolong this fancy, now the sense
Impels, the hour invites? Shall I not own
Such thoughts as women find to recompense
Their hidden lives when secret and alone?

Surprise the stranger in the heart, some strong
Young lion of the rocks who found his path
By night, and now he crouches all day long
Beside the pool to see me at my bath.

He would be there, a melancholy shade
Caught in the ambush of his reckless joy,
Afraid to stir for fear I call, afraid
In one unguarded moment to destroy

At once the lover and the thing he loves.
Who should he be? I cannot guess; but such
As desperate hope or lonelier passion moves
To tempt his fate so far, to dare so much;

Who having seen me only by the way,
Or having spoken with me once by chance,
Fills all his nights with longing, and the day
With schemes whose triumph is a casual glance.

Possessed by what he never can possess,
He forms his wild design and ventures all
Only to see me in my nakedness
And lurk and tremble by the garden wall.

He lives but in my dream. I need repel
No dream for I may end it when I please;
And I may dream myself in love as well
As dream my lover in the summer trees,

Suppose myself desired, suppose desire,
Summon that wild enchantment of the mind,
Kindle my fire at his imagined fire,
Pity his love and call him and be kind.

Now think he comes and I shall lie as still
As limpid waters that reflect their sun,
And let him lie between my breasts and fill
My loins with thunder till the dream be done.

The kisses of my mouth are his; he lies
And feeds among the lilies; his brown knees
Divide the white embraces of my thighs.
Wake not my love nor stir him till he please,

For now his craft has passed the straits and now
Into my shoreless sea he drives alone.
Islands of spice await his happy prow
And fabulous deeps support and bear him on.

He rides the mounting surge, he feels the wide
Horizon draw him onward mile by mile;
The reeling sky, the dark rejoicing tide
Lead him at last to this mysterious isle.

In ancient woods that murmur with the sea,
He finds once more the garden and the pool.
And there a man who is and is not he
Basks on the sunny margin in the full

Noon of another and a timeless sky,
And dreams but never hopes to have his love;
And there the woman who is also I
Watches him from the hollow of the grove;

Till naked from the leaves she steals and bends
Above his sleep and wakes him with her breast.
And now the vision begins, the voyage ends,
And the great phoenix blazes in his nest.

....Ah, God of Israel, even though alone,
We take her with a lover, in the flush
Of her desires. SUSANNAH!....I am undone!
What beards, what bald heads burst now from the bush!

Faustus

Laying the pen aside, when he had signed,
"I might repent, might yet find grace," he said,
"What could you do?" The Devil shook his head:
"You're not the first, my friend: we know your kind.

"Logic, not justice, in this case prevails:
This bond can't be enforced in any court.
You might prove false as hell, but have you thought
The fraud may damn you, though the promise fails?"

"Suppose I use these powers, as well I may,"
Said Faustus then, "to serve the cause of good!
Should Christ at last redeem me with his blood,
You must admit there'd be the devil to pay."

The Devil laughed and conjured from the air
A feast, a fortune and a naked bed.
"Suppose you find these powers use you instead!
But pun your way to heaven, for all I care.

"We could have had your soul without this fuss.
You could have used your wits and saved your breath.
Do what you like, but we at least keep faith.
You cheated God, of course; you won't cheat us."

Faustus unclasped the Book: when that first hour
Struck on his heart, a fragment broke away.
What odds? With four and twenty years to pay
And every wish of man within his power!

He asked to know: before the words were said,
Riddles that baffled Kepler all lay bare;
For wealth, an argosy walled in his chair;
For love, and there lay Helen in his bed.

Years passed in these enchantments. Yet, in fact
He wondered sometimes at so little done,
So few of all his projects even begun.
He did not note his will, his power to act

Wither, since a mere wish would serve as well,
His reason atrophy from day to day
Unexercised by problems, love decay
Untried by passion, desire itself grow stale,

Till he, who bought the power to command
The whole world and all wisdom, sank to be
A petty conjurer in a princeling's fee,
Juggling with spells he did not understand.

And when, at last, his last year came and shrank
To a bare month and dwindled to an hour,
Faustus sat shuddering in his lamp-lit tower,
Telling the time by seconds till time went blank.

Midnight had come: the fiend did not appear;
And still he waited. When the dawn began,
Scarce crediting his luck, he rose and ran
And reached the street. The Devil met him there,

It was too much. His knees gave way. He fell.
"The bond? ...My soul?" Quite affable, the fiend
Helped him to rise: "Don't fret yourself my friend.
We have your soul already, quite safe in Hell.

"Hell is more up-to-date than men suppose.
Reorganized on the hire-purchase plan,
We take souls by instalments now, and can
Thus save the fuss and bother to foreclose.

"And since our customers prefer, you know,
Amortized interest, at these higher rates,
Most debts are paid in full before their dates.
We took your final payment months ago.

"But, as I say, why fret? You've had your fun.
You're no worse off without a soul, you'll find,
Than the majority of human kind,
Better adjusted, too, in the long run."

Back in his tower Faustus found all bare.
Nothing was left. He called: the walls were dumb;
Drawing his knife, he stalked from room to room
And in the last he found her, waiting there,

That fabulous Helen his magic art had won.
Riches and power, she was their sum and prize;
Ten thousand years of knowledge were in her eyes
As first he cut her throat and then his own.

Advice to Young Ladies

A.U.C. 334: about this date,
For a sexual misdemeanour which she denied,
The vestal virgin Postumia was tried;
Livy records it among affairs of state.

They let her off: it seems she was perfectly pure;
The charge arose because some thought her talk
Too witty for a young girl, her eyes, her walk
Too lively, her clothes too smart to be demure.

The Pontifex Maximus, summing up the case,
Warned her in future to abstain from jokes,
To wear less modish and more pious frocks.
She left the court reprieved, but in disgrace.

What then? With her the annalist is less
Concerned than what the men achieved that year:
Plots, quarrels, crimes, with oratory to spare –
I see Postumia with her dowdy dress,

Stiff mouth and listless step; I see her strive
To give dull answers. She had to knuckle down.
A vestal virgin who scandalized that town
Had fair trial, then they buried her alive;

Alive, bricked up in suffocating dark;
A ration of bread, a pitcher if she was dry,
Preserved the body they did not wish to die
Until her mind was quenched to the last spark.

How many the black maw has swallowed in its time!
Spirited girls who would not know their place,
Talented girls who found that the disgrace
Of being a woman made genius a crime.

How many others, who would not kiss the rod,
Domestic bullying broke or public shame?
Pagan or Christian, it was much the same:
Husbands, St Paul declared, rank next to God.

Livy and Paul, it may be, never knew
That Rome was doomed; each spoke of her with pride.
Tacitus, writing after both had died,
Showed that whole fabric rotten, through and through.

Historians spend their lives and lavish ink
Explaining how great commonwealths collapse
From great defects of policy – perhaps
The cause is sometimes simpler than they think.

It may not seem so grave an act to break
Postumia's spirit as Galileo's, to gag
Hypatia as crush Socrates, or drag
Joan as Giordano Bruno to the stake.

Can we be sure? Have more states perished, then,
For having shackled the enquiring mind,
Than those who, in their folly not less blind,
Trusted the servile womb to breed free men?

Ode on the Death of Pius the Twelfth

To every season its proper act of joy,
To every age its natural mode of grace,
Each vision its hour, each talent we employ
    Its destined time and place.

I was at Amherst when this great pope died;
The northern year was wearing towards the cold;
The ancient trees were in their autumn pride
    Of russet, flame and gold.

Amherst in Massachusetts in the Fall:
I ranged the college campus to admire
Maple and beech, poplar and ash in all
    Their panoply of fire;

Something that since a child I longed to see,
This miracle of the other hemisphere:
Whole forests in their annual ecstasy
    Waked by the dying year.

Not budding Spring, not Summer's green parade
Clothed in such glory these resplendent trees;
The lilies of the field were not arrayed
    In riches such as these.

Nature evolves their colours as a call,
A lure which serves to fertilize the seed;
How strange, then, that the splendour of the Fall
    Should serve no natural need

And, having no end in nature, yet can yield
Such exquisite natural pleasure to the eye!
Who could have guessed in summer's green concealed
    The leaf's resolve to die?

Yet from the first spring shoots through all the year
Masked in the chlorophyll's intenser green,
The feast of crimson was already there,
    These yellows blazed unseen.

Now, in the bright October sun the clear
Translucent colours trembled overhead
And as I walked, a voice I chanced to hear
    Announced: The Pope is dead!

A human voice, yet there the place became
Bethel; each bough with pentecost was crowned;
The great trunks rapt in unconsuming flame
    Stood as on holy ground.

I thought of this old man whose life was past,
Who in himself and his great office stood
Against the secular tempest as a vast
    Oak spans the underwood;

Who in the age of Armageddon found
A voice that caused all men to hear it plain,
The blood of Abel crying from the ground
    To stay the hand of Cain;

Who found from that great task small time to spare:
– For him, and for mankind, the hour was late –
So much to snatch, to save, so much to bear
    That Mary's part must wait;

Until in his last years the change began:
A strange illumination of the heart,
Voices and visions such as mark the man
    Chosen and set apart.

His death, they said, was slow, grotesque and hard,
Yet in that gross decay, until the end
Untroubled in his joy he saw the Word
    Made spirit and ascend.

Those glorious woods and that triumphant death
Prompted me there to join their mysteries:
This Brother Albert, this great oak of faith,
    Those fire-enchanted trees!

Seven years have passed, and still, at times, I ask
Whether in man, as in those plants, may be
A splendour, which his human virtues mask
    Not given to us to see?

If to some lives at least there comes a stage
When, all the active man now left behind,
They enter on the treasure of old age,
    This autumn of the mind?

Then while the heart stands still, beyond desire
The dying animal knows a strange serene:
Emerging in its ecstasy of fire
The burning soul is seen.

Who sees it? Since old age appears to men
Senility, decrepitude, disease,
What Spirit walks among us, past our ken,
As we among these trees,

Whose unknown nature blessed with keener sense
Catches its breath in wonder at the sight
And feels its being flood with that immense
Epiphany of light?

The Planctus

Do quietem fidibus;
vellem ut se planctibus
sic possem et fletibus.
Abelard: PLANCTUS 6, IV, B.

I

Time be my Fulbert, history your Paraclete,
And Astrolabe though yours, not mine, alas!
Those two our palimpsest, we their looking-glass,
In essence, if not in accidents, complete;
No detail matches, yet the patterns repeat:
Thrice crows the cock as introit to the mass;
Buridan in his sack sees Buridan's ass
Stuck between wild oats and domestic wheat.

Were all their letters genuine? Who can tell?
Though ours authenticate the text at need,
Christ's cross for Adam's tree no more stands bail.
Tell-tale, tell-tale, tell-tale! tolls the bell,
While bill-boards outside Paradise now read:
"This Most Desirable Property, for Sale!"

96

II

The Faith is dead; the men are gone; their graves
Remain: these two byzantine churches and
The bones of those who built them. Silt and sand
Choked this proud city whose life was from the waves.
Lost Adam, lost Eve from a lost world, the nave's
Mosaics show us naked, hand in hand,
Fixed where now only tourists drift or stand,
The culture-addicts and the camera-slaves.

Who will remember our city in its grace?
Only ourselves, survivors, each inside
A separate ark, lost on the endless flood,
Posting each other at random on the wide
Waste waters, raven or dove to ask: What good
Will Ararat be, if Babel takes its place?

III

Angels of stone, great mountains, flash their brands
Of lightning round St Peter's tower, whose stone
Was cut when Peter, Berengarius' son
Was born; a house of grief not made with hands,
Set on that rock, is now my house; his lands
Of exile I inherit; the *Sic et Non*
Of mind and heart drags on; I sit alone
Petrus in vinculis...
                   suddenly his bands
Lie loose; a voice dispels the prisoner's sleep;
Domino suo... writes Heloissa's pen;
A *trouvère's* aubade finds his exiled King,
The lion-heart fretting in the Styrian Keep,
And this grey hillside glows as bright as spring
With autumn crocus and wild cyclamen.

97

IV

A horror of great darkness, in that dark
The furnace and the lamp between the slain
And lastly the Shekinah shining plain
Upon the friend of God, the patriarch.
I know the horror: I cannot find the friend;
I see the mysteries but I miss the light;
Bear with me now: against myself I fight:
Cannot go on, yet cannot make an end.

His enemies, when he visited her, would laugh
And say: the old Adam draws him to her still!
Fierce in his right he gave them all the lie.
Had he been in my case, had he known half
The agony of my divided will
Lama sabachthani must have been his cry.

V

My plane comes in to land and now I see,
As angels on their errands see, the bay
And Palo Alto and the Royal Way,
The hills beyond where grew our fatal tree.
Almost I could believe we stand there now
In that first flash of vision, when the eyes
Take in what still they cannot realize,
Our fingers meeting round its golden bough.

Ten years ago! A sorry angel, I,
Too late to an abandoned hearth descend.
The Palatine Peripatetic, having come
To such a point as this wrote: When I die
No matter where for my poor body send:
To that at least I shall not grudge its home!

VI

Dimisit eam: knowing it was too late
He preached on these two words from Genesis.
Abraham loved Sara still, he said, but his
Whole soul was Agar's, and, as they relate,
Having driven her out to satisfy the Lord,
His heart rebelled and grim for her distress
He ran to find her in the wilderness,
And met an angel with a flaming sword

Who said: Turn back! This desert was Paradise.
But showed him a well where Agar slept
Safe with her child. Far off a ghost crowed thrice.
Because he loved her more than all beside,
There Abraham fell upon his face and wept.
But Peter faced the brethren stony-eyed.

VII

In his last years, they say, a gentleness
Fell on this second Petrus, this rolling stone,
On whom, for all that, Thomas built the throne
Of doctrine. Peter of Cluny none the less
Was not deceived by this apparent peace.
He mourns beside the Burning Bush, he said,
That was his love. And, when the man was dead,
He sent the body back to Héloïse.

I am not gentle; I know (I shall not yield)
Time's rage; the cock may crow: I cannot weep;
This body rebels and lives, but moves apart
Not towards its Paraclete, but some Potter's Field.
Yet in your unconsuming flame, this heart
Rejoices and this spirit you have and keep.

VIII

Near death at St Marcel, he loosed his tongue.
Once when they asked his age, he said: I am
Older than wandering Caym, than Abraham
When he betrayed his love.... Yet I am young!
Seven years for Leah – they were years, no more;
The seven for Rachel were the seven days
Of the Creation, the renewal of grace
In that new testament beyond the law.

The seven that followed, and all that follow those
Cannot be told, for they are not in time
But in the eternal sabbaths of the song
I sent her for her nuns; for that I chose
A metre from the love-songs of my prime,
Since in that heaven of heavens all things belong.

Quis rex, quae curia, quale palatium,
Quae pax, quae requies, quod illud gaudium,
Hujus participes exponant gloriae,
Si quantum sentiunt possint exprimere.

IX (Epigraph)
PARADISE SAVED
(another version of the Fall)

Adam, indignant, would not eat with Eve,
They say, and she was driven from his side.
Watching the gates close on her tears, his pride
Upheld him, though he could not help but grieve,
And climbed the wall, because his loneliness
Pined for her lonely figure in the dust:
Lo, there were two! God who is more than just
Sent her a helpmeet in that wilderness.

Day after day he watched them in the waste
Grow old breaking the harsh unfriendly ground,
Bearing their children, till at last they died.
While Adam, whose fellow God had not replaced,
Lived on immortal, young, with virtue crowned,
Sterile and impotent and justified.

Moschus Moschiferus
A Song for St Cecilia's Day

In the high jungle where Assam meets Tibet
The small Kastura, most archaic of deer,
Were driven in herds to cram the hunter's net
And slaughtered for the musk-pods which they bear;

But in those thickets of rhododendron and birch
The tiny creatures now grow hard to find.
Fewer and fewer survive each year. The search
Employs new means, more exquisite and refined:

The hunters now set out by two or three;
Each carries a bow and one a slender flute.
Deep in the forest the archers choose a tree
And climb; the piper squats against the root.

And there they wait until all trace of man
And rumour of his passage dies away.
They melt into the leaves and, while they scan
The glade below, their comrade starts to play.

Through those vast, listening woods a tremulous skein
Of melody wavers, delicate and shrill:
Now dancing and now pensive, now a rain
Of pure, bright drops of sound and now the still

Sad wailing of lament; from tune to tune
It winds and modulates without a pause;
The hunters hold their breath; the trance of noon
Grows tense; with its full power the music draws

A shadow from a juniper's darker shade;
Bright-eyed, with quivering muzzle and pricked ear,
The little musk-deer slips into the glade
Led by an ecstasy that conquers fear.

A wild enchantment lures him, step by step
Into its net of crystalline sound, until
The leaves stir overhead, the bowstrings snap
And poisoned shafts bite sharp into the kill.

Then as the victim shudders, leaps and falls,
The music soars to a delicious peak,
And on and on its silvery piping calls
Fresh spoil for the rewards the hunters seek.

But when the woods are emptied and the dusk
Draws in, the men climb down and count their prey,
Cut out the little glands that hold the musk
And leave the carcasses to rot away.

A hundred thousand or so are killed each year;
Cause and effect are very simply linked:
Rich scents demand the musk, and so the deer,
Its source, must soon, they say, become extinct.

Divine Cecilia, there is no more to say!
Of all who praised the power of music, few
Knew of these things. In honour of your day
Accept this song I too have made for you.

On an Engraving by Casserius
For Dr John Z. Bowers

Set on this bubble of dead stone and sand,
Lapped by its frail balloon of lifeless air,
Alone in the inanimate void, they stand,
These clots of thinking molecules who stare
Into the night of nescience and death,
And, whirled about with their terrestrial ball,
Ask of all being its motion and its frame:
This of all human images takes my breath;
Of all the joys in being a man at all,
This folds my spirit in its quickening flame.

Turning the leaves of this majestic book
My thoughts are with those great cosmographers,
Surgeon adventurers who undertook
To probe and chart time's other universe.
This one engraving holds me with its theme:
More than all maps made in that century
Which set true bearings for each cape and star,
De Quiros' vision or Newton's cosmic dream,
This reaches towards the central mystery
Of whence our being draws and what we are.

It came from that great school in Padua:
Casserio and Spiegel made this page.
Vesalius, who designed the *Fabrica*,
There strove, but burned his book at last in rage;
Fallopius by its discipline laid bare
The elements of this Humanity
Without which none knows that which treats the soul;
Fabricius talked with Galileo there:
Did those rare spirits in their colloquy
Divine in their two skills the single goal?

"One force that moves the atom and the star;"
Says Galileo, "one basic law beneath
All change!" "Would light from Achernar
Reveal how embryon forms within its sheath?"

Fabricius asks, and smiles. Talk such as this,
Ranging the bounds of our whole universe,
Could William Harvey once have heard? And once
Hearing, strike out that strange hypothesis,
Which in *De Motu Cordis* twice recurs,
Coupling the heart's impulsion with the sun's?

Did Thomas Browne at Padua, too, in youth
Hear of their talk of universal law
And form that notion of particular truth
Framed to correct a science they foresaw,
That darker science of which he used to speak
In later years and called the Crooked Way
Of Providence? Did *he* foresee perhaps
An age in which all sense of the unique,
And singular dissolves, like ours today,
In diagrams, statistics, tables, maps?

Not here! The graver's tool in this design
Aims still to give not general truth alone,
Blue-print of science or data's formal line:
Here in its singularity he has shown
The image of an individual soul;
Bodied in this one woman, he makes us see
The shadow of his anatomical laws.
An artist's vision animates the whole,
Shines through the scientist's detailed scrutiny
And links the person and the abstract cause.

Such were the charts of those who pressed beyond
Vesalius their master, year by year
Tracing each bone, each muscle, every frond
Of nerve until the whole design lay bare.
Thinking of this dissection, I descry
The tiers of faces, their teacher in his place,
The talk at the cadaver carried in:
"A woman – with child!"; I hear the master's dry
Voice as he lifts a scalpel from its case:
"With each new step in science, we begin."

Who was she? Though they never knew her name,
Dragged from the river, found in some alley at dawn,
This corpse none cared, or dared perhaps, to claim,
The dead child in her belly still unborn,
Might have passed, momentary as a shooting star,
Quenched like the misery of her personal life,
Had not the foremost surgeon of Italy,
Giulio Casserio of Padua,
Bought her for science, questioned her with his knife,
And drawn her for his great *Anatomy*;

Where still in the abundance of her grace,
She stands among the monuments of time
And, with a feminine delicacy displays
His elegant dissection: the sublime
Shaft of her body opens like a flower
Whose petals, folded back expose the womb,
Cord and placenta and the sleeping child,
Like instruments of music in a room
Left when her grieving Orpheus left his tower
Forever, for the desert and the wild.

Naked she waits against a tideless shore,
A sibylline stance, a noble human frame
Such as those old anatomists loved to draw.
She turns her head as though in trouble or shame,
Yet with a dancer's gesture holds the fruit
Plucked, though not tasted, of the Fatal Tree.
Something of the first Eve is in this pose
And something of the second in the mute
Offering of her child in death to be
Love's victim and her flesh its mystic rose.

No figure with wings of fire and back-swept hair
Swoops with his: Blessed among Women!; no sword
Of the spirit cleaves or quickens her; yet there
She too was overshadowed by the Word,
Was chosen, and by her humble gift of death
The lowly and the poor in heart give tongue,

Wisdom puts down the mighty from their seat;
The vile rejoice and rising, hear beneath
Scalpel and forceps, tortured into song,
Her body utter their magnificat.

Four hundred years since first that cry rang out:
Four hundred years, the patient, probing knife
Cut towards its answer – yet we stand in doubt:
Living, we cannot tell the source of life.
Old science, old certainties that lit our way
Shrink to poor guesses, dwindle to a myth.
Today's truths teach us how we were beguiled;
Tomorrow's how blind our vision of today.
The universals we thought to conjure with
Pass: there remain the mother and the child.

Loadstone, loadstar, alike to each new age,
There at the crux of time they stand and scan,
Past every scrutiny of prophet or sage,
Still unguessed prospects in this venture of Man.
To generations which we leave behind,
They taught a difficult, selfless skill: to show
The mask beyond the mask beyond the mask;
To ours another vista, where the mind
No longer asks for answers, but to know:
What questions are there which we fail to ask?

Who knows, but to the age to come they speak
Words that our own is still unapt to hear:
"These are the limits of all you sought and seek;
More our yet unborn nature cannot bear.
Learn now that all man's intellectual quest
Was but the stirrings of a foetal sleep;
The birth you cannot haste and cannot stay
Nears its appointed time; turn now and rest
Till that new nature ripens, till the deep
Dawns with that unimaginable day."

The School of Night

What did I study in your School of Night?
When your mouth's first unfathomable yes
Opened your body to be my book, I read
My answers there and learned the spell aright,
Yet, though I searched and searched, could never guess
What spirits it raised nor where their questions led.

Those others, familiar tenants of your sleep,
The whisperers, the grave somnambulists
Whose eyes turn in to scrutinize their woe,
The giant who broods above the nightmare steep,
That sleeping girl, shuddering, with clenched fists,
A vampire baby suckling at her toe,

They taught me most. The scholar held his pen
And watched his blood drip thickly on the page
To form a text in unknown characters
Which, as I scanned them changed and changed again:
The lines grew bars, the bars a Delphic cage
And I the captive of his magic verse.

But then I woke and naked in my bed
The words made flesh slept, head upon my breast;
The bed rode down the darkness like a stream;
Stars I had never seen danced overhead.
"A blind man's fingers read love's body best:
Read all of me!" you murmured in your dream.

"Read me, my darling, translate me to your tongue,
That strange Man-language which you know by heart;
Set my words to your music as they fall;
Soon, soon, my love! The night will not be long;
With dawn the images of sleep depart
And its dark wisdom fades beyond recall."

Here I stand groping about the shores of light
Too dazzled to read that fading palimpsest.
Faint as a whisper that archaic hand

Recalls some echo from your school of night
And dead sea scrolls that were my heart attest
How once I visited your holy land.

As Well as They Can

As well as it can, the hooked fish, while it dies,
Gasping for life, threshing in terror and pain,
Its torn mouth parched, grit in its delicate eyes,
    Thinks of its pool again.

As well as it can, the poet, blind, betrayed
Distracted by the groaning mill, among
The jostle of slaves, the clatter, the lash of trade,
    Taps the pure source of song.

As well as I can, my heart in this bleak air,
The empty days, the waste nights since you went,
Recalls your warmth, your smile, the grace and stir
    That were its element.

A Mu'allaqat of Murray's Corner

*"Estás así distante, así lejos de mi misma amada como si habrías sido muerta
antes de mi nacimiento, o bien no ya nacida de mi viva.
Mas estás aquí, te veo a ti, así es como tendrías el tamaño de un gigante o el de
una muñeca."*

— LA MUÑECA VIVA

This is the place, friend, strange to your eyes, no doubt,
So used to the treeless, harsh Arabian waste;
Valleys bare as an ass's belly, granite flanks of Mt. Yadhbul;
Here the young mountain stream winds in and out
Through she-oaks and eucalypts under Murray's Hill
Planted with pines to the top; from pool to pool
It chuckles and gushes, easily, without haste

Making its way to the gorge where it leaps to the plain.
Even at midday in summer the place is cool,
Secret and shaded, sunlight dapples the still,
Small, rockbound reaches. Here, like gentle rain
Or like the ghost-voice of an ancient sea
Which covered these hills once, casuarina and pine
Answer each other; cicadas sizzle with long
Hot, sleepy, stridulent bursts of song,
Evoking that lost world of a year ago.
High up the mountainside, there comes to me
The archaic lament of a solitary crow.

Here we laid out our picnic: a bottle of wine,
Sandwiches, a few black olives, a bunch of grapes.
I lay on my back and drank in the leaf-patterned-sky.
The talk of the world went through us like the shapes
Of cloud and tree, the voice of the stream. Our own
Talk drifted, stopped, went on, like the design
Of our cigarette smoke on the air. The hours went by
And I moved into her arms and seemed to flow
And melt into her elemental air like the talk, like smoke.
Then nothing was left but our bodies, each to each
Talking together their exquisite, ultimate speech,
Till they, too, were silent and only the silence spoke.

For you Imr al-Qais, whose Suspended Ode is the cause
I brought you here, a fourteen-centuried ghost,
For you, who trapped Unaiza and her virgins once all day
Naked in Dāra Juljul's pool, and after
Slaughtered your camel to feast them, and they tossed
The red meat, frilled with fat, to and fro in their play,
For you who crept into her litter and had your way,
This, perhaps, would have been an occasion for laughter;
For you, who made each post a winning post,
An occasion for boasting. You would be wrong, my friend,
Yet would recognise, perhaps, better than most,
My joy: the spirit of one content to snatch
An ephemeral happiness, worth all the rest
Of living and more regretted in the end.
Men set their hearts on things that last; they test

109

Time by the rule of time; cannot see that there is
Sometimes a leap beyond its level to catch
Heaven in the epiphany of a kiss,
An interstitial moment that masters time,
Gives all things their meaning, present or past
And brings the uncertain soul to its senses at last.

If you look very carefully at this bank you will see
The prints our bodies made in the grass that day;
If you scan these weaving shadows, the interplay
Of limbs still tracing the patterns of their caress;
If you listen, holding your breath, you may still hear
Our voices, a murmur of laughter, the archaic sea
Resonant yet, like a shell held to the ear,
Though the waters have vanished; and, if you lie down and press
Your face to earth, you will feel the throb, the thud
Of two hearts beating the measured dance of the blood.

Why do I tell you this, brother? I bring you here
To help me find an answer. Some days ago
She came to tell me she is to marry. I said
"It makes no difference: all that we shared, we share."
And this was the truth. She is with me everywhere,
Bone of my bone; the great conversation goes on
Deep down, whatever change the surface may show.
Yet the hour she left me, that assurance had fled.
The world was empty. We had drunk the last of the wine.
Though I wished her well as before: no difference, no!
Love towards the living may pass into love for the dead
Unchanged – but death is the difference. And the loss.
Though we talk to *them*, no answer crosses that line;
We should find no-one there if *we* were able to cross.

That is why I come, my ghostly friend, like a ghost
Myself, and bring you here to visit this place,
To bear me witness, to find myself again.
I hold there are moments of time that cannot be lost
And places like this in which they remain and bless.
Few things live on in their causes, hidden or plain,
But those where the heart comes home, where the heart says: Yes!
Yes, now and here!, these always bless and remain.

I have returned to myself, Imr al-Qais, even as you
When you wept at the camping site between Ad-Dakhūl
And Haumal among the dunes and looked for the trace of her fire,
The marks of her tent still there, scattered with antelope dung.
Bear with me now: I have been all kinds of a fool,
But an old fool is the worst, when the woman is young.
There are many modes of love: it translates into every tongue,
But there is one does not: the root of desire
Is the search for yourself in another who looks for herself in you.
It may not happen at all – strange if it did for strangers
Who wander in time and space so vast, so tiny our range is,
That our chances of meeting are less than collision of stars, and
    less
Than the odds against life emerging on any planet.
And yet we are *here*; the unpredictable chance
Does happen once in an unpredictable while;
The inscrutable visage of God redeems us with a smile.

She might have been born in a different nation, another
Age. I have loved some who spoke
From another century: Emily Brontë was one;
Heloissa was one; Laila al-'Akhyalīyaħ, another!
I think of *La muñeca viva*, the lover who woke
To find the incredible true, the matching one
Beside him, sharing his bed, sharing the wonder
Of recognition, the unmistakable glance
Of meeting eyes, of meeting spirits – and still
There was that gulf between to keep them always asunder:
He was a full-grown man and she too small to fill
The palm of his hand. It made no difference at all.
They were the lucky ones, they had met against all the odds.
So I think of myself, how blest I am to be here,
To have lived for one year in the blessing of God's smile.
I might have missed it forever; indeed I was late to the feast;
But coming at all, I count myself a fortunate man at least.
Two stars in their courses approach, then retreat beyond recall
Yet nothing is lost, if within that millionth mile
They know what they are by the chance of that millionth year.

As for us, Imr al-Qais, we did not pass within hail.
That is one thing that more than most I regret;
I have met no man in my time like you; and yet
There is another knowledge in which we meet:
The endurance of rock, the will to resist and prevail;
Whatever life does, to choose one's own way and rejoice.
Remember the desert, the wolf in the stony dale
Howling his hunger and you, in the wolf's own voice
Answering, laughing: "That makes two of us friend!"
A fierce, wild pitiless wolfish man, you set
No bounds to your love, nor to your hate; you did
Not deny the world and took it for what it is,
But sang it; and, though it broke you, rejoiced to the end.
You were born in the Jāhilīya; the light was hid
From your eyes; yet the *amīr al-mūminīna*
Hung your ode in the House, gave it pride of place,
Written in letters of gold, set in the eye of God,
That splendid, intractable, scandalous pagan ode;
A parable for the poets whose nomad race
Glorify God in the words of the Opening Prayer:
Iyyaka na'budu wa Iyyaka nasta'inu!

Come, friend, we must be going. We thought to share
The last of the wine, but the wine will always be there;
From that unbelievable, necessary part
Of life that is not part of living its fountains start.
Nothing is lost, though brightness should fall from the air.

Pervigilium Veneris

Ovid and Pushkin, Byron and Ronsard,
Gongora, Goethe, poets past thinking of,
Poets who played Love's game and played it hard
    – They were never out of love –

Age did not daunt them; even the last eclipse
Found them still eager, still adding to the score.
Scholars in their chaste dens, pursing their lips,
      Tally as they deplore.

The romantic, the censorious may condemn
Their greedy, untidy lives. I do not doubt:
Their genius and their gift of love, for them
      Were of a piece throughout.

Women flocked to them; their part in the divine
Was bringing their living waters in pitcher or urn,
Knowing the water would be changed to wine,
      Sure that they could return,

And, in their household task, the rearing of men
And women, the precious chrism would not be lost.
The poets forgot them; they returned to the pen
      And thought themselves star-crossed.

Neither of their divine gifts was denied:
Assured by the rule that holds in love and war,
Apollo their source, Aphrodite their guide,
      And Zeus their avatar.

Clover Honey

Father first noticed it: "Upon my Sam,
This soil breeds spinsters! Five miles round, I swear,
Live twenty old maids – not that *I* give a damn,
But Mary and Susan here might have a care.

"Daughters are perishable goods at best;
At worst – Yes, dear, I *do* know when to stop –
But twenty at church today! Who would have guessed
So rich a shire could raise that blighted crop?"

113

Susan just giggled; I totted up Father's count:
"Nineteen is what I make it, not twenty, Dad!"
"You've missed our gruesome help here, Sarah Blount,
"Haven't you, girl? Admit it!" – and so I had.

"By God!" – he flourished his carvers in the air –
"She makes my flesh creep. No one asks *my* advice
Of course; but how your mother puts up with her
Passes my – yes, dear! yes, another slice?"

Susan and I discussed it later in bed.
"Father was horrid to laugh; he doesn't *know*!
If I don't marry," said Sue, "I'd rather be dead."
I laughed too: "Well, we've both some years to go."

But for all that, I brooded on their lives;
Imagined them as young girls like me or Sue;
Tried to imagine them happy mothers and wives
And wondered what went wrong – though mostly I knew.

Rumour, in country places, rarely leaves
Misfortune a shift or nakedness a clout.
At Tea-cup Time, when Gossip brings home her sheaves,
The skeletons rattle in closets for miles about.

Miss Tabitha and Miss Mildy at the Grange
Had been too high and mighty, people said;
Miss Prue had beauty, but no one thought it strange:
Papa had lost his money. The suitors fled.

Miss Martha had offers too. They had to wait –
A bed-ridden mother – and, as is often the case,
When free to marry, she found it was too late;
Miss Claire's club-foot cancelled that angel face.

Poor, gay Miss Belle never got her man to church;
There was Miss Madeleine, too – but never mind,
Too simple, too yielding: he left her in the lurch.
It's an old story, and people are so unkind.

Miss Sophie was unattractive from the start;
Miss Tetty, of course, had always been a shrew;
But why Miss Constance with her loving heart
Had never married, not even our gossips knew.

Eighteen is an uncompromising age.
Old maids, fag-ends of living, cat-fanciers,
I thought of them with mounting pity and rage
And blamed the order of the universe.

My father's friend – he lived near us in Kent –
A Mr Darwin, used to visit our house,
And when I raged at him in protest, sent
A twinkle at me from his beetle brows:

"Yes, yes, poor things!" he said, "You have a heart
That does you credit, my dear. But let me say
That the great chain of being has found a part
In Nature's scheme even for them to play.

"You mentioned cats, I think. Each keeps a cat?"
"Good God!", I said, "they have them by the score!"
"Indeed? Of course, I'm not surprised at that;
But cats catch mice – Well, it's what cats are for.

"Their mistresses at night will put them out
To hunt for field-mice – You begin to see
My drift, perhaps, since as you know, no doubt,
The field-mouse preys upon the bumble-bee.

"These hirsute bees, and they alone, contrive
To fertilize the dark red-clover blooms;
Although it is their smaller cousins who hive
The clover-honey that loads our Kentish combs.

"So when we find – what does the Bible say? –
A land flowing with milk and honey, we do
Not doubt, we naturalists, that there we may
Expect to find old maids a-plenty too.

"The state of single blessedness, you see,
Is not without its talent; indeed, you might
Call spinsters partners of the honey bee
Bringer of life's best gifts, sweetness and light."

Times change; old maids now in these parts are rare.
That would have made Mr Darwin smile, because
I hear old farmers here in Kent declare
The honey-flow is nothing like it was.

I did not marry, myself. As I recall
I have never had reason to complain of that.
Susan was wed, poor Sue, three times in all;
But now we live together. We keep a cat.

Eyes and Tongues

*– mea gaudia narret,
dicetur si quis non habuisse sua.*

Sulpicia

Take me, dear heart, you said, and think no blame;
Let the world whisper; let them pry and stare;
    If children at their play
On streets, on walls with yours chalk up my name,
What matter? We may laugh at laughing spies.
If in our innocence we trusted then
To walk as angels do, unseen by men,
Pillared at night in fire, in cloud by day,
    Yet from the first we were
    Ringed round with tongues and eyes.

Love was a babe newborn, still pure from sin;
We could not guess what our first glance implied;
    Yet someone standing near
Then nudged his neighbour with a knowing grin.
We had scarce exchanged that first, strange hesitant kiss,
Alone, by night, when rumour wagged his head

116

And busy tongues had brought us both to bed.
What wonder, since the candle shone so clear,
  What hope, indeed, to hide
  So royal a blaze as this?

So if their mouths speak ill of us, my heart,
And custom dog us, jealous in his right,
  Heart, do not be distressed.
Think, in Love's commonwealth all have a part:
Some to command, some to base tasks are born;
As some are thieves by nature, some must prate
From natural malice and traduce the state.
Princes know this, yet do not break their rest
  But sleep in spite of spite
  And rise refreshed at morn.

Let them say what they will. To love, to live
Is our great office, place and priesthood too.
  We hear, but as we move
Through all the murmuring gossip of the hive,
Myriad eyes may glitter with ill-will;
Myriad stings flick out, yet, turned to us
Their tongues dip in our honey; what they discuss
Tastes sweet and they are nourished by our love.
  They know not what they do,
  But are forgiven still.

Say more: say, love refines them with the flame
Of pentecost; they speak as men possessed;
  Our seventh heaven awhile
Catches them up. This fellow who cries shame
Drinks ecstasy. Though with scorn his lip is curled,
He is our witness now and not our spy;
And that shrill she, if love has passed her by,
As some report, yet walks with us her mile
  And, by that company blest,
  Shares in our better world.

The Invaders

Coming by night, furtively, one by one,
They infiltrate according to the Plan,
Their orders memorized and their disguise
Impenetrable. With the rising sun
Our citizens welcome them. Nobody can
Think that such charming creatures might be spies.

So feeble, so helpless, no one could suspect
They come to make this commonwealth their prey;
So few, they pose no threat; their cohort grows
So imperceptibly that we neglect
To notice how it musters day by day
And, unalarmed, we watch as they impose

Themselves, make friends in all directions, take
Impressions of all keys. They gain access
To all our secrets; learn to speak our tongue
Like natives; profit by each false move we make;
Work on our weaknesses; observe and guess
The sources of power and study them to be strong.

And when it happens, there will be no fuss,
No streets running with blood, no barricade.
We shall simply wake one morning to discover,
As those who ruled this city before us
Found by each door a headstone and a spade,
That a new generation has taken over.

Speak, Parrot!
Monon Calon Agaton
Quod Parato
In Greco

Speak, parrot, speak, flamboyant popinjay!
Speak, though like me you've nothing new to say;
Repeat what I repeated yesterday,

Equally pleased for cracknels to rehearse
Wisdom or prophecy or immortal verse
Or trivial chatter or a filthy curse.

In ages past, though now it seems absurd,
Once you were thought the Bearer of the Word;
Princes paid ransoms for the speaking bird;

Hermetic syllables scattered from your beak;
Great scholars, who even dreamed in Attic Greek,
Were hired to gloss whatever you might speak;

The Laureate poets, honoured by your state,
Would bite a golden phrase off short and wait
Patient to hear the orient fowl orate;

Because, they said, you hailed from Paradise,
The legend grew that parrot never dies:
Poets, too, once had their immortalities.

Speak, parrot! Tell me, would you rather be
A mindless oracle or a man like me
Grubbing in the dry springs of poetry?

Well, at Time's door we make a pair, my friend:
Both transmit what we scarcely apprehend;
Poets are not so different in the end.

Hay Fever

Time with his scythe honed fine,
Takes a pace forward, swings from the hips; the flesh
Crumples and falls in windrows curving away.
Waiting my turn as he swings – (Not yet, not mine!)
I recall the sound of the scythe on an earlier day:
Late spring in my boyhood; learning to mow with the men;
Eight of us mowing together in echelon line,

Out of the lucerne patch and into the hay,
And I at the end on the left because I was fresh,
Because I was new to the game and young at the skill –
As though I were Time himself I remember it still.

The mild Tasmanian summer; the men are here
To mow for my minister father and make his hay.
They have brought a scythe for me. I hold it with pride.
The lucerne is up to my knee, the grass to my waist.
I set the blade into the grass as they taught me the way;
The still dewy stalks nod, tremble and tilt aside,
Cornflowers, lucerne and poppies, sugar-grass, summer-grass,
     laced
With red-stemmed dock; I feel the thin steel crunch
Through hollow-stalk milk thistle, self-sown oats and rye;
I snag on a fat-hen clump; chick-weed falls in a bunch,
But sorrel scatters; dandelion casts up a golden eye,
To a smell of cows chewing their cuds, the sweet hay-breath:
The boy with the scythe never thinks it the smell of death.

The boy with the scythe takes a stride forward, swings
From the hips, keeping place and pace, keeping time
By the sound of the scythes, by the swish and ripple, the sigh
Of the dying grass like an animal breathing, a rhyme
Falling pat on the ear that matches the steel as it sings
True through the tottering stems. Sweat runs into my eye.
How long to a break? How long can I hold out yet?
I nerve my arms to go on; I am running with, flooding with, sweat.

How long ago was it? – Why, the scythe is as obsolete now
As arrows and bow. I have lived from one age to another;
And I have made hay while I could and the sun still shone.
Time drives a harvester now: he does not depend on the weather.
Well, I have rolled in his hay, in my day, and now it is gone;
But I still have a barn stacked high with that good, dry mow,
Shrivelled and fragrant stems, the grass and the flowers together
And a thistle or two in the pile for the prick of remorse.
It is good for a man when he comes to the end of his course
In the barn of his brain to be able to romp like a boy in the heap...
To lie still in well-cured hay...to drift into sleep.

The First-born

Sanctify unto me all the firstborn, whatsoever openeth the womb among the children of Israel, both of man and of beast: it is mine.

Exodus 13 : 2

There is something different about them. Almost all
Voices of eldest children give them away.
– I know; I am one myself of that secret clan –
They have listening faces; their stance, their steps recall
A guarded alertness from an earlier day
Far back in the dangerous history of man.

They cannot help it: it is a fear inbred
From times when the first-fruits were offered up
To ravenous gods. More precious than ram or goat
Was a first-born son on an altar dripping red;
And a first-born girl exposed on the mountain top
Felt the wolf's muzzle, hairy against her throat.

These cannot take life for granted as others do.
They shrink from kinship and kind; they have learned to greet
A kiss with caution, joy with a settled calm;
A celebration warns them they are taboo
And a caress reminds them that human meat
Torn at the summer solstice becomes a charm.

No matter what nonchalance he may command,
This one betrays at times the furtive eyes
Of a lost fugitive from some sacred grove;
This other, a still unsacrificed deodand,
Even in her rapture, a lover may surprise
Some anxious gesture at the climax of love.

Whatever opens the womb of men or beasts
Is sacred to Moloch's or Jahweh's holy writ:
Weak from her birth-pangs, a girl mother comes,
Milk still oozing from her swollen breasts,
And hurls her first-born into the fiery pit
Its sole shriek drowned by the wild gongs and drums;

121

And, walking with joy in the clear mountain air,
A young boy laughing, the beloved son,
Skipping and chattering at his father's side,
Touches the sacrificial knife: "But where,
Where is the victim?" – Abraham, trudging on,
Groans out: "God knows, my son, let God provide."

Spätlese

A late picking – the old man sips his wine
And eyes his vineyard flourishing row on row.
Ripe clusters, hanging heavy on the vine,
    Catch the sun's afterglow.

He thinks: next vintage will not be too bad.
The *spätlese* at last, as I recall,
Has caught the grace I aimed at as a lad;
    Yet ripeness is not all.

Young men still seek perfection of the type;
A grace that lies beyond, one learns in time.
The improbable ferment of the overripe
    May touch on the sublime.

Old men should be adventurous. On the whole
I think that's what old age is really for:
Tolstoy at Astapovo finds his soul;
    Ulysses hefts his oar.

For David Campbell
And, lo, they were very dry.
Ezekiel, XXXVII.2.

At the Last Judgement, as the final batch
Is sorted out: "Goats, seventeen; sheep, three!"
God may permit himself at last to snatch
A yawn or two; then, looking at his watch:
"TIME, Gentlemen, please! Henceforth Eternity!"

At which, well pleased, with a decisive clap
Recording Angel will shut up his book,
And Devil's Advocate, dog-tired, poor chap,
Take off his horns, put on his halo, wrap
His nimbus round, when someone bawls: "Hey, look!

"Hold it! There's someone coming up the street!"
And sure enough, far down that dusty slope
Trod by so many million shuffling feet,
A straggler comes in view. God takes his seat,
Saying, "I might have known it: Alec Hope!

"Always the tail-end of the bloody mob;
Always too feckless even to cut it fine.
The Foolish Virgins did a proper job
Compared with him; well, when that loafing slob
Arrives, we'll really lay it on the line!"

"Wait, Lord! He does not come alone, though," cries
The D.A. putting back his horns and tail.
"One in, all in's the rule!" The Lord replies,
"Contempt of court will fit them all for size,
And just don't let me hear you ask for bail!"

And round the last bend weaving up the straight,
Glorious, hilarious, erratically slow,
The company of the incorrigibly late,
Campbell and Hope approach the Pearly Gate
Passing a long-necked bottle to and fro.

God bends his ireful brows upon the pair;
Singles me out: "Well, Alec Hope, you have
Ten seconds flat, I say, ten seconds bare,
If either of you have anything to declare
Against the bottomless pit, the fiery grave."

"Well, Lord, there's little enough that I can say;
We met this morning after the final crunch,
(The Resurrection, I mean) and thought the way
To celebrate Damnation and the Last Day
Would be to give ourselves a splendid lunch."

"Lunch!" says the Lord, "You poets beat the band!
Lunch on a day like this? My Day of Doom!
You keep ME waiting, and you turn up canned;
What can you possibly...?" "Lord, you understand,
We poets develop a grand thirst in the tomb

"We've been a long time dead; our bones were dry
As those Ezekiel in his vision raised up.
And there were these new tongues of ours to try
For wine and song – Well, David Campbell and I
Resolved to make a halt for bite and sup.

"We met outside the Bacchus too. In short
He said: 'Look, Alec, this seems the finger of Fate;
Why don't we...?' 'Dave,' I said, 'the selfsame thought
Occurred to me. My turn to shout though, sport;
I've owed you a lunch since nineteen sixty-eight.'

"'Ten centuries?' he said: 'Well, what d'you know?
That's quite a time for building up a thirst.
We mustn't forget, of course, there's a big show
At Heaven's Gate today – we've got to go,
But what I always say is: First things first!

"'Besides, there's something more: I think I've got
A poem coming on.' 'For that a fine
Pokolbin, David, would be just the shot;
And Heaven will be dry as like as not.'
Well that's our story, Lord, Campbell's and mine."

"Campbell?" the Lord will say, "Now let me see;
He's a good poet and always dead on time.
I'd put this lapse down to bad company.
We're short of poets in Heaven too...Dear me,
He wouldn't, by any chance, have finished that rhyme?"

"Just what he did, Lord! You should hear it, you should!"
And Dave will speak those lines at Heaven's Gate
And God will say: "Well done, Campbell, jolly good!
Let's hear more, Campbell, while we're in the mood.
Let Time continue: Eternity can wait!"

There in a listening silence the world will end
With poetry as with poetry it began
And, when it is done, the Lord will smile and bend
His eyes on me and say: "Well, Hope, your friend
Has saved your bacon; at least I think I can

"Just stretch the rules a little – So, on your way!
Get along, both of you; and don't forget:
There'll be no lunching in Heaven from today;
Pick up your harps from Peter, and learn to play;
We'll expect some heavenly music from you yet."

The Mayan Books

Diego de Landa, archbishop of Yucatan
– The curse of God upon his pious soul –
Placed all their Devil's picture-books under ban
And, piling them in one sin-heap, burned the whole;

But took the trouble to keep the calendar
By which the Devil taught them to count time.
The impious creatures had tallied back as far
As ninety million years before Eve's crime.

That was enough: they burned the Mayan books,
Saved souls and kept their own in proper trim.
Diego de Landa in heaven always looks
Towards God: God never looks at him.

In Memoriam: James Philip McAuley, 1976

Sleep sound here, brother, by your tranquil bay!
What can the tongue we both served now express
Other than this? all that is left to say
    Is loss and emptiness,

Empty as ocean stretches towards the pole
Beyond this island which you loved, my friend,
This island where at last you reached your goal
    Of landfall at Land's-end;

This island which your lucid poet's eye
Made living verse: wildflower and sedge and tree
And creatures of its bushland, beach and sky
    Took root in poetry,

Until a world to which your poet's mouth
Gave being and utterance, country of the heart,
Land of the Holy Spirit in the South,
    Became its counterpart.

It was my island too, my boyhood's home,
My "land of similes"; from all you gave,
This I hold close and cherish, as I come
    To your untimely grave.

Where the great mount's apocalyptic beast
Now guards your bones and watches from the height,
Fixing his lion gaze towards the east
    For the return of light,

Standing on this last promontory of time,
I match our spirits, the laggard and the swift;
Though we shared much beside the gift of rhyme,
    Yours was the surer gift.

Your lamp trimmed, full of oil, you went before,
Early to taste the Bridegroom's feast of song;
Wait for me, friend, till I too reach that door;
    I shall not keep you long.

The Drifting Continent

Black Mountain. Summer. All those years ago,
As though no further back than, say, last week,
That meeting of mammal with monotreme comes to mind.
The mountain above us, the parched plain below,
We sat in the dry gully of a dry creek;
I, picnicking with a female of my kind;

Two recent mammals, perhaps the last of all,
The strangest and most generalized, at least,
We shared our sandwich lunch, poured out our wine;
The air was shrill with locusts, I recall;
Ants and the pestering bush-flies joined our feast;
She sat and held her hairless paw in mine.

The ancient land enfolded us; our talk
Turned to its arid earth, the history
Of its archaic inhabitants adrift
On its pre-Cambrian shield and later rock,
Of their long isolation on the sea,
Progressing by that imperceptible shift,

Two centimetres a year, or so they say,
Mounted upon the great tectonic plate
On which it floats upon the mantle below,

127

And of ourselves, frail creatures of a day,
Yet the sole animal to contemplate
The irony of its own fierce urge to know.

"What other mammal recalls its past," I said,
"But man and can remember all others too?"
She laughed and said: "The Geophysical Year
Made possible that dialogue with the dead.
As for *our* place upon this drifting zoo,
Remember we are interlopers here.

"Placental mammals on marsupial ground,
We are trespassers on their continental raft
Inching its way up from the pole," said she;
"But, though no fossil record has been found,
There was an older crew aboard this craft
Before those first marsupials put to sea.

"Before it set out from Gondwanaland,
Perhaps two hundred million years ago,
The earliest of mammals, or the last
Of links with bird and reptile held command
And this was monotreme country then, although
They vanished leaving no trace upon the past.

"But two of them survive, the only two,
To help us guess what once they must have been.
One is the duck-billed platypus and one
The spiny ant-eater..." As if on cue,
As she broke off, far down the dry ravine
A creature moved from shadow into sun;

And at its shuffling pace the echidna came
Towards us from the immemorial past
(We watched and held ourselves as still as death),
Pausing to lick up ants and such small game.
"Here comes a member of your crew, at last,"
I muttered to my friend below my breath.

She did not speak or nod, but watched it quest
Slowly along the dry creek's sandy bed.
It seemed to waddle upon its powerful claws,
Here lifting a stone, scouring a meat-ant's nest
Turning from side to side its bird-like head.
Yet, though it seemed so often to loiter and pause,

It shambled level with us before we knew,
Halted and peered about with purblind eyes,
And seemed to sense, although it could not see,
The creatures on the bank. It sniffed my shoe
And snuffled; we saw the momentary rise
Of quills along its back; then quietly

Out of the pipe-like mouth a worm of tongue
Flickered and tasted all along the welt
And, as though puzzled, it stood there deep in thought
Till, having considered, it went its way along
The creek and round a bend. It must have felt
A tremor through the subsoil of some sort

Or heard me as I leapt to follow, for
Fast as I turned the corner, it was gone.
And yet how could it? The ravine ahead
Was bare and clear for fifteen yards or more.
I looked for hole or burrow: there was none.
Then my companion following laughed and said:

"Try looking by your feet!" And when I did
The sandy floor before me was astir
With points of spines: echidna had dug in
So fast that in five seconds it was hid.
"Best leave him to himself," I said to her,
"At least we have seen the race of mammals begin."

She answered: "But it could have been a dream.
We are too ephemeral to comprehend
Such motion as your continental drift.
Perhaps this meeting, for the monotreme,
Was no beginning, but presaged the end.
Man's landing on their raft was dire and swift.

"How many of its old crew have vanished, say,
As this one in the sand before your feet?
How many species since seventeen eighty-eight,
When *we* first came upon this transport, may
Already count their massacre complete
(Outside the central deserts, at any rate)?"

"Man looks before and after," I replied,
"I wonder where this curious ark is bound
And who, of all its internecine crew,
Will man it when, born on the magmal tide,
On a more massive raft it runs aground,
As sister India is said to do?

"My bet's on the echidna, before man.
Man is too greedy to survive for long,
Needs far too many gadgets to succeed;
Echidna needs no more than ants and can
Get by with no technology but its tongue.
When man has perished, with all that served his greed,

"I see our drifting continent arrive,
Echidna and the ants alone on board.
– Some of man's ruins, perhaps, for what they're worth."
"Or if he wins, perhaps *no* creature alive
May make that landfall when, not fire and sword,
But effluents and his filth have killed the earth.

"Should life renew itself in time to come,
Some new intelligence may find it moored
Against a young uplifted mountain crest,
Or still adrift, and wonder at the doom
That overtook its crew; like those aboard
That sea-enigma, the *Mary Celeste*."

"Mary of Heaven, great mammary mamma,
Star of the Sea, to whom all mammals pray,
Will she protect us yet?" I asked. We laughed
Questioning, should we invoke an older star,
A more archaic saint who, in their day
Blessed monotremes and piloted their craft.

We laughed, but with a deep and growing unease.
We had lost our human assurance of thought and speech.
The elemental silence deprived our breath;
Lost in the tale of all those centuries,
We were no longer persons, each to each,
But ciphers in a species bound for death.

Beware of Ruins

Beware of ruins: they have a treacherous charm;
Insidious echoes lurk among their stones;
That scummy pool was where the fountain soared;
    The seated figure, whose white arm
Beckons you, is a mock-up of dry bones
And not, as you believe, your love restored.

The moonlight lends her grace, but have a care:
Behind her waits the fairy Melusine.
The sun those beams refract died years ago.
    The moat has a romantic air
But it is choked with nettles and obscene
And phallic fungi rot there as they grow.

Beware of ruins; the heart is apt to make
Monstrous assumptions on the unburied past;
Though cleverly restored, the Tudor tower
    Is spurious, the façade a fake
Whose new face is a death-mask of the last
Despairing effort before it all went sour.

There are ruins, too, of a less obvious kind;
I go back; cannot believe my eyes; the place
Is just as I recall: the fire is lit,
    The table laid, bed warmed; I find
My former world intact, but not, alas,
The man I was when I was part of it.

Inscription for a War

Stranger, go tell the Spartans
we died here obedient to their commands.
    Inscription at Thermopylae

Linger not, stranger; shed no tear;
Go back to those who sent us here.

We are the young they drafted out
To wars their folly brought about.

Go tell those old men, safe in bed,
We took their orders and are dead.

Romancero

Ambushed by some wild Basques at Thornydale
A baggage-train perishes in the Pyrenees –
So Einhard in his *Life of Charlemagne* –
Three centuries pass. A poet retells the tale;
Roland's disaster, riding home from Spain,
Becomes more glorious than most victories.

History gives way to epic, as it should;
Heroic deeds from commonplace facts are born.
Still down the centuries, echoing from the steep,
As the long, desperate day goes down in blood,
Resound the dying notes of Roland's horn.
But man's imagination cannot sleep;

Epic in turn gives way to high romance;
The epic poets at most replaced a few
Basque bandits by that countless Saracen host,
A mere task force by the twelve peers of France;
But with the poets of romance is lost
All sense of the fantastic or the true;

And Durandal, great Durandal, the sword
Which Roland in the epic could not break,
Now in romance becomes a valiant Knight
Who fell at Roncesvalles beside his lord;
And Montesinos who survived that fight
– Unknown to epic – was at first a snake.

Things flow, things drift, things swirl and change like mist!
Belerma, O Belerma, what were you
Before you fondled Durandarte's heart,
Cherished nine years and handled, mourned and kissed?
Were you, perhaps, your lover's counterpart:
Belle Aude's bare bodkin and her poignard too?

Ruidera next, six daughters and a niece
Or two, so wept at Durandarte's grave
That Merlin, who by now was in the act,
Turned them, all nine, into a pond apiece.
Don Quixote had it told him for a fact
By Montesinos in his magic cave.

Three centuries of scholarship with its frost
Nipped back those tender crops of a new age
And ruined the harvest of Cervantes' day.
Epic, romance, each in its turn, was lost
And, pure research having restored his page,
Now sober History is here to stay.

Truth, as they say, is great and shall prevail.
I have no quarrel with that; but what of Rhyme
Whose truth is vision, whose task to guard the pass
With Roland or seek with Galahad the Grail?
For those who gaze in her enchanted glass,
Time has an end whose end is not in time.

Lot's Wife

But his wife looked back from behind him, and she became a pillar of salt.
Genesis 19 : 26

And the Just Man walked behind the envoy of God
Huge and radiant, along the dark hill-track;
But her anxiety spoke to his wife aloud:
"It is not yet too late; you could still look back

"Upon your native Sodom and its red towers
The square you sang in, the courtyard where you span
The blank windows of that tall house of yours
Where you bore children to your beloved man."

She looked – and froze in mortal agony,
Her eyes were sightless from that instant forth,
Her body became transparent salt and she
Stood with her swift feet rooted in the earth.

Who will mourn for this woman? Who will rue
Nor think her the least part of that mischance?
My heart at least will not forget her, who
Gave up her life just for a single glance.

Thirsty Paddocks
(from the Greek Anthology)

Thirsty paddocks drink the rain;
Trees drink from the earth again;
Ocean drinks the rivers first;
Sun from ocean slakes his thirst;
Last, the moon when all is done,
Drinks her splendour from the sun.
In a world so given to drink
Why then, comrades, should you think
Me a sot and call me sinful
When I try to get a skinful.

134

Frémito do meu corpo a procurarte...
(from the Portuguese of Florbela Espanca)

Quiver of my body reaching out to you,
Fever of my hands upon your skin intent,
With amber, vanilla, honey redolent,
My eager arms, wild to enfold you too.
Eyes searching to meet your eyes everywhere,
A thirst for kisses – bitterness of gall –
A hunger harsh and cruel that nothing there,
Nothing can ease or satisfy at all.
I see you far from me! your spirit near
I sense like a lake-water calm and clear
That says to me singing: You, I do not love...
And my heart, for which you feel no desire,
Goes floating at random, as the currents move,
A black skiff on a boundless sea of Fire.

Möbius Strip-Tease

An erudite demon, a fiend in topology,
Shaped much like a grin on a sphere on a trivet,
To add to the carnal advancement of knowledge he
Invented a woman. Now, would you believe it?

A woman so modelled no man could resist her,
So luscious her curves, so alluring her smile,
Yet no daughter of Eve's could claim her for sister,
Though equally formed to seduce and beguile.

For her surface – a pure aphrodisiac plastic –
No mathematician could ever equate
By any contortion or motion elastic
To those we caress in man's fallen estate.

O she was a heartache! O she was a honey!
The fiend asked his friends gathered round in a ring:
"A degenerate set! Would you bet even money,
Though she looks like a succubus fit for a King?"

"Come off it," they answered, "her shape is a woman's,
So she can't be a true topological freak,
Though a singleton, maybe, to ordinary humans
Who think any girl they adore is unique."

"In our rubber sheet world," said the fiend with a chortle
Converting himself to a three-masted barque,
"Equivalent shapes may delude a poor mortal,
But *you* should know Woman's distinguishing mark."

"A woman's a man-trap," they answered in chorus,
"A trochus with trunnions, a tunnel to Hell;
Reduced to essentials she's simply a torus
And this must apply to your temptress as well."

"Alas, my poor friends you are sadly mistaken:
This exquisite creature is built to deceive;
For the Devil's own cunning will not save his bacon
When caught in the nets that topologists weave.

"This marvellous manifold's not like a doughnut,
Quoit or cat's-cradle or twists of red tape,
And though very tortive, she screws like no known nut;
So I'd better explain her remarkable shape.

"Like a Boy Surface girl, my delightful invention
In Euclidean space is too awkward to plot,
But in Hell, with the help of an extra dimension
And a regressive cut, she's a true-lovers'-knot,

"Though she looks like a woman from thrutch-piece to throttle,
If you follow my clew of a Möbius strip-tease,
She is really a camouflaged double Klein bottle
With only one surface unlike other shes.

"Four Möbius strips brought my plan to fruition,
Ingeniously joined by original sin;
If you rise to the urgings of male intuition,
You'll find yourself out every time you go in.

"She cannot be mated or orientated,
Nor is homeomorphic to any known male;
And though in her arms you may feel quite elated,
All further advances are destined to fail.

"And before we proceed to our first Demon-stration,
May I venture to say, with excusable pride,
That this elegant essay in total frustration
Justifies mathematics, both pure and applied.

"Furthermore, as a torment for sinful seducers,
I think I may claim for the very first time,
To have added to Hell's repertoire something new, sirs:
A case where the punishment *won't* fit the crime."

Glossary for Non-Mathematical Demons

TOPOLOGY	A field of Botany invaded by certain mathematicians with a sense of humour; devoted to studying the shapes of things.
MÖBIUS, KLEIN & BOY	Topologists of great eminence and a profound sense of humour.
ELASTIC MOTION	The imaginary shift of spatial points required to change one spatial shape to a mathematically equivalent shape. Also something girls do without any mathematical knowledge at all.
DEGENERATE SET	A coarse logical term for a class of things containing only one member; a member of the class of classes of unique individuals; a mathematical term of abuse.
SUCCUBUS	A theological entity, rather than a mathematical one; if you don't know what it is, you'd better not worry your pretty little head about it.
SINGLETON	see "degenerate set": nothing to do with bridge.
RUBBER-SHEET-WORLD	Topology (for topologists), otherwise something out of Grimm to help Frog Princes to bed.
TROCHUS	Anything in the shape of a wheel; in topology it might be a lot of other things as well.
TRUNNIONS	Arms (or legs) of a cannon barrel.
TORUS	A refined (or mathematical) word for anything shaped like a doughnut.
MANIFOLD	A connected surface such that if you caress it, it will respond by being thigmotactic to your hand – such as a girl or a football.
TORTIVE	Twisty or twistable, according to your intentions.

BOY SURFACE	A very sophisticated three-dimensional figure with only one surface. Invented by Mr Boy (see Möbius, Klein etc).
REGRESSIVE CUT	A mathematical way of getting your own back and making some surprising discoveries on the way.
THRUTCH-PIECE	Consult a very big dictionary; it probably won't help you, but your imagination may.
MÖBIUS STRIP	What happens when you twist your belt putting it on. It has only one side and one edge and numerous even more remarkable properties.
KLEIN BOTTLE	An attempt to make two Möbius strips copulate without benefit of more than three dimensions; A hell of a topological joke.
ORIGINAL SIN	Not a mathematical operation as far as can be proved – but you never know.
MALE INTUITION	Not a mathematical idea either, but it has associations with binary arithmetic.
ORIENTATED	You wouldn't understand this anyway – a topological technicality.
HOMEOMORPHIC	Topologically equivalent in shape.
DEMON-STRATION	Just an ordinary demo, but conducted in another place.
THE CRIME	See "Original Sin".

Printed in the United Kingdom
by Lightning Source UK Ltd.
131439UK00001B/61/A